11/99 11/08

THE EARLY VICTORIAN WOMAN

"THE IDEAL EXPECTED . . . DELICACY AND MODESTY, A SMALL
WAIST AND CURVING SHOULDERS" *(Chapter* I)

[JENNY LIND]

Mezzotint

From the author's collection

The
Early Victorian Woman

Some Aspects of Her Life
(1837–57)

by

JANET DUNBAR

George G. Harrap & Co. Ltd
London   Toronto   Wellington   Sydney

To
C., L., AND F.
AND IN MEMORY OF P.

First published in Great Britain 1953
by GEORGE G. HARRAP & CO. LTD
182 High Holborn, London, W.C.1

Dewey Decimal classification: 396

*Composed in Garamond type and printed by
Western Printing Services Ltd, Bristol. Made in Great Britain*

PREFACE

I HAVE called this book *The Early Victorian Woman*, but the first thing I must ask myself is: Which early Victorian woman should I take for my subject? The 'amusing' caricature of revue? The crinolined mama surrounded by a dozen children? The courageous pioneer who fought for the higher education of women and the beginnings of civil rights for them? The wretched sempstress, sewing by candlelight: the half-naked, brutalized woman in the coal-mine: the domestic servant in her basement: the nail-maker and chain-maker and slaving factory-hand? They were all the Early Victorian Woman, and it is impossible to think of one without remembering the others.

Much has been written about the Victorian period, that age of prejudice and progress, of exploitation and awakening social conscience. Embedded in the histories one catches glimpses of daily life at different social levels. Volumes of memoirs depict leisured women sitting on lawns or conversing brilliantly at dinner-parties. The fashion journals of the day mirror a world of luxury, beauty, and grotesqueness. The biographies of outstanding women show what extraordinary courage and perseverance were needed to make an impression on public opinion over anything which concerned women's emancipation. And, grimmest picture of all, the reports published by Government commissions into the conditions of the "industrial and perishing classes" give some idea of the lives of working-class women in factory and mill.

I wanted to know something of a woman's everyday life during the first twenty years of Victoria's reign, and I was fortunate enough to be given permission to read old diaries, letters, housekeeping account-books, and other papers belonging to private families; my material is taken from these, as well as from journals and newspapers of the time.

It is the middle-class woman who inevitably emerges from a study of the period: the familiar figure who has become, for us, the symbol of Victorian respectability. The journals published especially for her instruction and amusement devote a good deal of space to domestic matters and fashion and gossip, to what Thackeray called "yon fribble"; but they also published solid articles on theology, philosophy, science, literature, and the arts. In an age when the average woman could not get any real education she was able to keep herself well-informed by reading.

A good deal must have been going on behind many a housewifely façade during the period which I have taken as a frame, 1837–57. It was a time when the rising prosperity of the middle classes should have made for increased comfort and security, and therefore for women's contentment with their lot. It was, in fact, a period when the frustrations and discontents of women came to a head below the surface of life, and presently broke through. Wives began to question Authority, both in the home and in the State. Spinsters decided that it was time they were allowed to use whatever intellect they were blessed with, and to be given the opportunity of an education and a chance to enter the professions. Mrs Bloomer preached the gospel of rational dress and showed her legs—suitably covered, of course. Women were reminded that freedom from whalebone armour was just as possible as freedom from the tyranny of other conventions.

Some copied Amelia Bloomer; most disapproved of her "trowsers." But, though they clung to their massed skirts, they were ready to listen to new ideas in other fields. When the pioneers of higher education for women and the early advocates of women's franchise addressed meetings they were sure of crowded audiences. Women were turning towards any opportunity of increasing their knowledge and of using their intelligence and initiative outside the sphere of home life.

They needed intelligence and initiative inside that sphere

too. We are apt to think of the Victorian woman as repressed and without a personality of her own. The reverse is true. She was the centre of the home, and it needed a good many positive qualities to run that little world. Sometimes those qualities had to include cunning, and a hard-headed business sense, to enable her to hold her own in a society where she was denied elementary civil rights.

The majority of women accepted their bondage with more or less graceful resignation, relying on affection and a sense of duty to carry them through life. We shall see something of the rebels later, and of the outstanding women who began movements which were to change the course of social history. Let us start with the average young woman, born into the end of one era, and growing up to womanhood in the first twenty years of Victoria's reign.

My first thanks are due to Mr Robert Owen, who encouraged me to begin this book.

I am greatly indebted to the Women's Service Library, Westminster, and to their Librarian, Miss Vera Douie, for putting at my disposal their unique collection of books, journals, manuscripts, and original letters relating to women's life and work in the early nineteenth century, and for much help and advice as to source material.

I also record with appreciation the assistance I have had from the staffs of the British Museum Reading Room, the Victoria and Albert Museum Library, and Mr Gilbert Turner, Librarian of the Richmond (Surrey) Public Library, and his staff.

I wish to thank Lord Auckland for giving me access to valuable material relating to Emily and Fanny Eden; Messrs the W. B. Saunders Company, Ltd, for allowing me to quote a passage from Garrison's *Introduction to the History of Medicine*; and Messrs Methuen and Co., Ltd, for permission to quote from *Under Five Reigns*, by Lady Dorothy Nevill, and from *Records and Reminiscences*, by Sir F. C. Burnand.

I am also indebted to Mrs Bernard Croft-Murray for allowing me to reproduce her Leech drawing, and to Mr

Edward Croft-Murray, of the British Museum, and Mr James Laver, of the Victoria and Albert Museum, for help and advice about prints of the period.

Mrs Doris Langley Moore generously showed me her magnificent collection of period clothes at a time when she was busy preparing her Museum of Costume; and among others who have been of great assistance I must mention Mr Victor Crosse, Mrs Mary Howard, Miss Ruth How, Mrs J. C. Evans, Mr William Morrell, and Mr Stanley Crowe.

My thanks are also due to the British Broadcasting Corporation for permission to include in the book material which has already been used as a basis for broadcast talks and other programmes.

J. D.

CONTENTS

PART I: THE HOME BACKGROUND

XIV: OUTSTANDING WOMEN

XV: TOWARDS EMANCIPATION

ILLUSTRATIONS

PART 1

THE HOME BACKGROUND

I

MARRIAGE

WE begin where many novels leave off, with marriage. The author of a book on feminine perfection wrote in 1840, "A female's real existence only begins when she has a husband," and this was the normal early Victorian view. A girl had few illusions on the matter. Marriage, 'getting settled,' was her aim; any other future was bleak.

Jane Austen had stated the case plainly when she gave Charlotte Lucas's reasons for accepting Mr Collins; and though this was written forty years before Victoria came to the throne it was still valid for the average Victorian young woman:

"Marriage had always been her object; it was the only honourable provision for well-educated young women of small fortune, and, however uncertain of giving happiness, must be their pleasantest preservative from want."

The fact that marriage, besides being a pleasant preservative from want, also brought with it the most astounding disabilities, was taken for granted, or at least accepted. A woman's children, her property and earnings, all belonged to her husband by law. It took the case of Mrs Caroline Norton, with its aura of scandal in high life, to catch the attention of the public, and to make known what tragedies could be caused by the inequalities of these laws. But we shall hear more of Mrs Norton.

Of course, not all, or even most, women of the early

B

Victorian period married for convenience and put up with husbands for the sake of having a home. Love-matches were as common in those days as they have always been. Arranged marriages, however, were not unusual in the middle classes, and there is much evidence to show that they were often very happy.

The early Victorian girl was a realist. She satisfied her romantic longings by reading the primly passionate novels of the time, but she married suitably, either a man of her own or her parents' choice. The question of marriage or a career did not arise in the middle and upper classes. When Florence Nightingale refused an offer of marriage and insisted on studying the conditions in hospitals instead Mrs Nightingale was genuinely bewildered as well as angry. She could not conceive such an attitude of mind.

Florence Nightingale was an exception. The majority of young women hoped they would marry, and prepared accordingly, ably aided by their mothers. They set about it in a thoroughly sensible and practical way. They read books on the subject:

"Just out, Price 1s.: *How, When, and Whom to Marry*, with Observations on the Causes of Marriage being so often Unhappy."

"*The English Wife*, a Manual of Home Duties, designed as a sequel to *The English Maiden*. Cloth 4s. 6d., silk 6s. The Young Wife will find herein the Proper Rules, not only for securing her husband's affection, but also for conducting her establishment."

The earnest and popular authoress Mrs Ellis had some advice to give under the heading "Dealing with a Husband" in her book *The Women of England*, published in 1839. Discussing the man who liked to go out in the evening without his wife, she said:

"The rational woman, whose conversation on this occasion is to serve her purpose more effectually than tears, knows better than to speak of what her husband would probably consider a most unreasonable subject of complaint. She tries to recollect some incident, some trait of character, or some anecdote of what has lately occurred within her knowledge, and relates it in her most lively and piquant manner. If conscious of beauty, she tries a little raillery, and plays gently upon some of her husband's not unpleasing peculiarities, looking all the while as disengaged and unsuspecting as she can. If his attention becomes fixed, she gives her conversation a more serious turn, and plunges at once into some theme of deep and absorbing interest. If her companion grows restless, she changes the subject, and again recollects something laughable to relate to him. Yet all the while her own poor heart is aching with the feverish anxiety that vaccilates between the extremes of hope and fear. She gains courage, however, as time steals on, for her husband is by her side, and with her increasing courage her spirits become exhilarated, and she is indeed the happy woman she had hitherto but appeared; for at last her husband looks at his watch, is astonished to find it is too late to join his friends, and while the evening closes in, he wonders whether any other man has a wife so delightful and entertaining as his own."

There is no doubt these books were read and their precepts taken to heart; but there must have been many young Victorian women who enjoyed *Punch's* advice in the matter, given in the early forties:

"Between ourselves, my dear, almost every young woman is either married or intends to be. It is what we have to look to, poor things! Now, in order to get married, my love, you must learn to manage yourself; and after you get married, you must learn to manage your husband; and both together is what I call the Whole Duty of Woman.

"As long as you are single and looking out, your first duty must be to control your inclinations. All of us, you know, have our little failings; the great thing is to conceal them. For instance, suppose you have a hearty appetite, you should restrain this a little in company, as it is a thing many gentlemen object to; and you can indemnify yourself by a nice supper in your own room. You will then please the kind of men who make the best husbands—those most easily managed.

"If, my dear, you have any personal blemish, which you

think would prevent a certain person from liking you, hide it from him if you can, and let him find it out after you are married.

"Never contradict him, dear, but fall in with all his little wishes and whims, however unreasonable. In short, devote yourself to him entirely. Your turn will come."

But for every girl who appreciated the jibing pen of the then-radical *Punch* there were a hundred who were more at home with *La Belle Assemblée* and other journals of fashion. Making the most of one's charms was a very serious business. Since getting a husband was the only way of becoming respectably settled in life, a girl had to try to reach an ideal of feminine perfection.

That ideal was laid down by men, and writers like Mrs Ellis made it quite clear what was expected: softness and weakness, delicacy and modesty, a small waist and curving shoulders, an endearing ignorance of everything that went on beyond household and social life. Husbands did not as a rule require brains in their wives; they demanded charm, a high sense of domestic duty, admiration for and submission to themselves, and the usual accomplishments necessary for entertaining friends.

Together with all this were the ever-increasing demands of etiquette and convention imposed by women themselves. The standard was set by the Royal young wife at Windsor, and most people felt that it was high time a standard *should* be set. The preceding thirty years had seen family life and national morality sink to a low ebb. It was hoped that Victoria's accession to the throne, followed by her marriage, would mark the beginning of a new age in personal conduct. This hope forms the core of an indictment on waltzing contained in *The Ladies' Pocket Book of Etiquette* (1840):

"The popularity of the waltz can be attributed to the iniquity which pervaded in high places, at the time of its introduction. At that time, there being no Queen, the morals of the Court became corrupt; the strict propriety, for which the Court of Queen Charlotte was so celebrated, disappeared during the reign of her son, and the place of the matrons of the best of our nobility became vacant, to admit

"THE QUEEN AND PRINCE ALBERT'S POLKA"

(Song cover)

From a lithograph by J. Brandard

By courtesy of the Director of the Victoria and Albert Museum

CAROLINE NORTON
From a lithograph by T. Fairland after F. Grant, A.R.A.
By courtesy of the Director of the Victoria and Albert Museum

A SCENE ON THE LAKE, FROGMORE
From a lithograph in the Cannan Collection
By courtesy of the Trustees of the British Museum

21

the titled courtezan and parasite. This, then, was the time and the season for the introduction of the waltz . . . the most degenerating dance that the last or present century have seen. It is, however, to be hoped, that the good sense, good taste, and delicate feelings of our young and good and gracious Queen, will dismiss this impurity from the Court." The age of respectability had set in.

It might seem, looking back, that the pendulum began to swing a little too far in the opposite direction. People quickly—too quickly—became decorous to the outward eye. Hypocrisy? We cannot tell. It is difficult for the average person, and especially the average woman, not to conform to the conventions. The Victorian wife, or the girl hoping to be a wife, had to conform to many conventions in the young Victoria's day, especially as the Queen had absorbed her consort's German ideas of what a good wife should be, and expected others to follow her example. The influence of the Court was very strong, especially on the middle classes. The girl who hoped that some gentleman might 'offer' had a great deal to prepare for, both in attempting to live up to the ideal he demanded and in keeping abreast of the social and domestic laws which complicated existence.

She had also to guard against being thought 'clever.' There was a good deal of reaction against the blue-stockings of earlier days—that group of cultivated women who, at the end of the eighteenth century, had enjoyed the friendship of men of intellect on equal terms. Times were changing. It wasn't the business of a girl who hoped to marry to be 'clever.' Marriage meant exchanging the authority of a father for that of a husband. How could one submit to unquestioned authority if one had the ability to argue rationally?

Thackeray had a different mind on the matter. This is what is said to Bob Brown in *Letters to a Young Man about Town*:

"Well, tell us about this girl. Is she a clever woman? I would rather like to see you fall to the lot of a clever woman. A set has been made against clever women from all times. Take Scott's ladies, and other writers: each man seems to draw from one model. An exquisite slave is what we want for the most part; a humble, flattering, smiling, tea-making, pianoforte-playing being, who laughs at our jokes however old they may be, coaxes us and wheedles us in our humours, and fondly lies to us through life.

"There are many more clever women in the world than men think for. Our habit is to despise them; we believe they do not think because they do not contradict us, and are weak because they do not struggle and rise against us. A man only begins to know women as he grows old; and for my part, my opinion of their cleverness rises every day."

Having achieved marriage, a girl took on a dignity and authority which has no counterpart in marriage as we know it to-day. The position of the married woman of those days can best be seen against the general attitude towards the spinster. Early marriages were the rule, and an unwed woman of thirty was already an object of pity. She took her place in the family as an unsuccessful human being, and, though she might be loved and respected by all the house-hold, a bitter drop of condescension was generally mixed with the affection. She became the aunt, the nurse, the useful member of the family who had no responsibilities of her own, the person whom the others could call upon for help in any emergency.

The married woman, by contrast, had a status, a position in society. She had become the mistress of a household, and she was able, for the first time, to give orders to servants and tradesmen on her own responsibility, and to make decisions for herself instead of having to obey her parents. This new-found power often brought out a strong personality in a hitherto quiet girl, and marriage must sometimes have been an unexpected and adventurous affair for many a new Victorian husband who had been used to well-disciplined sisters at home.

The young married woman settled down to establish the solid Victorian home which has become legendary; but there were some aspects of her new life which we should find intolerable, but which she had to accept as the natural order of things.

The first was the general conditions of childbirth. Having children was attended by the most ghastly risks of infection. It is an unceasing wonder that so many women survived and that families were so large. One comes upon revealing entries in old family papers: "Dear Emily expired an hour after our second son was born. I am excessively grieved. . . ." "Mr Throston married his third wife last Monday. His two previous ladies died in childbed, poor things. . . ."

No official records of maternal mortality were kept in those days, but there is a mass of evidence to show that untrained and incompetent midwives must have been responsible for countless deaths of mothers and babies. Dickens did not overdraw the type in Sarah Gamp. There were attempts to rouse public opinion to the dangers of employing such women, but it was not a subject that could be debated publicly, and little was done to preach the gospel of hygiene. The young wife was made to understand that there were mysteries which must be left in the hands of older, more experienced women—which meant, in effect, that she must place herself in the hands of Providence and hope for the best.

Most of the medical men of that period seem to have been indifferent to strict cleanliness in childbirth cases, judging by their opposition when anyone tried to put into practice new ideas in this field. Here is an instance of what two pioneer doctors had to face:

"Oliver Wendell Holmes read to the Boston Society for Medical Improvement his paper, *On the Contagiousness of Puerperal Fever*, in which he affirmed that puerperal fever was highly contagious, and that washing hands in calcium chloride and changing the clothes after leaving a puerperal fever case was likely to be a preventive measure. Holmes' essay stirred up violent opposition. . . .

"In 1855, he returned to the charge in his monograph, *Puerperal Fever as a Private Pestilence*, in which he reiterated his views, and stated that a Hungarian, Ignaz Philipp

Semmelweis, an assistant in the first obstetric ward of the Algemeines Krankenhaus in Vienna, had lessened the mortality of puerperal fever by disinfecting the hands with chloride of lime and a nailbrush. Semmelweis instituted such precautions in the handling of labour cases that the mortality curve sank from 9.92 to 3.8 per cent., and in the following year sank to 1.27 per cent.; and all through the simple expedient of washing the hands in a calcium solution in connection with pregnancy and the conduct of labour. Semmelweis is thus the true pioneer of antiseptics in obstetrics. . . . He put up a stiff fight for his ideas. . . and in future will be one of medicine's far-shining names, for every child-bearing woman owes something to him."[1]

Anæsthetics in childbirth were unknown until about 1846, when James Simpson first used ether for the mother in delivering a child. Simpson was a well-known young Edinburgh doctor who specialized in obstetrics. He took a close interest in the experiments then being made in America of the use of sulphuric ether in dentistry, and he made the first trial of its effect in midwifery. The results were so encouraging that he made further experiments, and presently developed the use of chloroform in childbirth, as chloroform did not require the cumbersome apparatus necessary for the administration of ether.

Simpson's discoveries roused jealous opposition in his profession, and prejudice and hostility in many people, including women themselves. They thought the use of anæsthetics 'not natural.' Suffering was considered to be an inevitable prelude to the joys of maternity, and any alleviation of it must be flying in the face of Providence.

There were women, however, who voiced the opposite point of view. Fanny Kemble, writing home from America at about the time her first child was born, said:

"I cannot believe that women were intended to suffer as much as they do, and be as helpless as they are, in childbearing. In spite of the third chapter of Genesis, I cannot believe that all the agony and debility attendant upon the entrance of a new creature into life was ordained." In

---

[1] F. H. Garrison, *An Introduction to the History of Medicine.*

editing this passage some years later she commented: "The beneficent action of ether had not yet mitigated the female portion of the primeval curse when I wrote those lines."

Simpson was undaunted by the opposition he met, and continued to develop the use of anæsthetics in midwifery practice. Many of the ladies of the aristocracy were not slow to benefit by the new discovery, and one finds it mentioned in journals and memoirs of the late forties. Queen Victoria had chloroform in two of her confinements, and that led to its wider popularity. But the practice did not reach the majority of wives: they continued to have their babies without the benefit of anæsthetics.

As women took this state of affairs in their domestic life for granted, so they accepted their place in the wider sphere of public life. They had no legal status of any kind in that sphere. Their position was the same as it had been when Blackstone stated in his *Commentaries on the Laws of England*, in 1765:

"By marriage, the very being or legal existence of a woman is suspended, or at least it is incorporated or consolidated into that of the husband, under whose wing, protection or cover she performs everything, and she is therefore called in our law a feme covert."

As 'feme covert' simply means 'married woman,' Blackstone was saying that the term 'married woman' indicated a woman who had no existence in common law apart from her husband. It meant that she could not sue anybody, nor be sued, nor be called as a witness. It also meant that she could lose the company of her children; her husband could take them from her if he wished, no matter what kind of character he had. Any property she owned or inherited became his as a matter of course, and if she earned any money, that belonged to him too.

The worst legal disability for a woman was the fact that she could not be released from a bad husband, no matter how cruelly he treated her; for a woman could not easily obtain a divorce before 1857. Theoretically it was possible before that date, but it required a special Act of Parliament, *lower class.*

and for those without money or influence it was almost hopeless to sue.[1]

In 1857, after a great deal of persistent work by a small body of men and women, a Bill was brought forward to make divorce accessible through the law courts and not through Act of Parliament. There was a tremendous uproar over this attempt to tamper with family life. The newspapers were filled with strongly worded articles and editorials, some for the Bill, more against it. One journal declared that the Bill jarred with poetical notions of wedlock; another said that women were developing a disquieting desire for equality with men.

The Bill went through; a fuller account of its passage is given in a later chapter. The new Act, with several amendments, remained basically the law concerning divorce until well into the twentieth century. But it was still undreamt of by the Victorian woman of our period, and so we return to the thirties and forties and fifties, when marriage was a life-sentence of happiness or unhappiness—or, as was more usual, a mixture of both.

We have been talking so far of marriage in the middle classes, of the girl whose aim in life was to have an establishment of her own and the status of a married woman.

The working-class girl had the same ideas about status, but marriage usually brought for her little change in her hard existence, unless it was the necessity to labour even longer hours than she had done before. If she married a factory-hand she usually kept on with her work in order to add her pittance to her husband's low wages. That meant twelve to sixteen hours in a mill or other factory, with neither the time nor the ability to make a home in the real sense of the word. She seldom knew anything about cooking or running a house; small wonder, since she had probably been working in shop or factory from the age of ten.

The commissions appointed by Parliament in the thirties

---

[1] In 1839, however, the Custody of Infants Act gave the mother a right to appeal to the courts, which could give her access to her infant children, or even their care if under seven.

and forties to inquire into the effects of factory work on women and girls make this point again and again. In 1843 the report of one commission stated:

"The employment of females during childhood prevents them from forming the domestic habits usually acquired by women in their station. Few can sew, bake or cook; a vast number of these females cannot make or mend, or repair a single tear. A girl who has been accustomed for years to a manufactory cannot cook a dinner of the plainest description. In consequence, the man she marries has no home but the beer shop."

The girl who married a farm-labourer or blacksmith and lived in the country at least enjoyed pure air and could get country food. She had to learn to cook at an early age, for there were no shops at which she could buy the pies and prepared dishes—many of them of doubtful value—on which her counterpart in town relied so much. The young country housewife was mainly responsible for the family food-supply; she cured the bacon, looked after the poultry, made bread, churned butter, and was ready to help the farmer's wife or to assist in the kitchens of the local manor-house when she was needed.

This was in addition to the domestic work of a cottage where water was pumped from a well, and light came from cheap candles or from colza oil lamps which had to be wound up as well as cleaned and filled. When her family came along she scarcely stopped work to attend to the babies; they had to be fitted somehow into her endless day.

The country wife knew from childhood that this was what marriage meant in her station of life. There were few pleasures. The pedlar came round with his pack of knick-knacks, and the Fair brought a little colour and music into her life when it arrived at the village once or twice a year. She made the most of weddings and christenings and festivals, of which accounts have come down to us in homely local journals. Here is an advertisement from a Northern newspaper in the late forties:

"JOLLIFICATION! Farmer Dale has with good heart lent his field alongside the river for the yearly Jollification of his Men and their Relations. All are welcome with their families."

One likes to imagine that Farmer Dale's men thought to ask some of their relations who worked in the factory towns nearby, and that there were wives among them who could take a husband's arm for at least one free working-day, and wander by the river, and taste the ease and idleness enjoyed by the fortunate women on the rung above them in Victorian society.

II

HOME AND FAMILY

Foundations of Family Life: Myth and Reality—The Husband's Rights—
Child-care and Nurture—Minor Ailments and Remedies—Home Education
—Family Games and Amusements

THE Victorian home has grown into a myth for our
generation. Some think of it with horror as a prison in
which sensitive children were bound by chains of duty
and obedience. Elizabeth Barrett's home is taken as a pro-
totype of the early Victorian home, and her father as the
typical Victorian head of a family; though her home was
exceptional, and Edward Moulton Barrett would have been
a psychopathic case in any period. Charlotte Brontë's works
throw into harsh light the tyranny, the hypocrisy, the pom-
pousness which were characteristic of the worst side of early
Victorian life.

To balance the picture one must read much farther. The
biographies of Mrs Gatty and Mrs Ewing give a far truer
understanding of the relationship between parents and
children; the lives of the Gurneys of Earlham, of Caroline
Fox, of Barbara Leigh Smith, of Octavia Hill, and the lesser-
known women who have left diaries and letters and journals,
give some idea of the warmth, the security, and affection of
family life, as well as the limitations.

It is difficult for us, over a hundred years later, to look at
early Victorian home life objectively, because we take for
granted so many freedoms which the Victorian woman did
not possess. Above all, our values are so different. The
early Victorians, reacting from the raffish Regency period,
became earnest and conventional; and we laugh at both

these attitudes. They were religious; and we are suspicious of piety, equating it with hypocrisy.

This last is an arrogant assumption. We may despise the snobbishness and intolerance of both the Established Church and the Nonconformists which drew sharply defined divisions between them; we may smile at the serious discussions on 'doubts' which fill so many journals. We may frown at the stupid way in which religion was so often presented to children, and be filled with pitying anger that Christina Rossetti could give up happiness with the man she loved because he had different religious convictions from her own. But we must recognize that religion was a real and tremendous force in Victorian family life, in spite of the fact that it was often paraded and conventionalized.

Morally over-earnest the early Victorians may have been, but they were also sincere in their beliefs—as were those who reacted from religion. The rationalists, the agnostics, those who could not accept the current creeds, were, for the most part, passionate adherents of the humanitarian ethic. It was not a religious belief, but it *was* a belief in goodness. Family life had the solid foundation of a standard outside itself, whether of religion or humanitarianism.

The pattern was, of course, the young Queen and her steadily filling nursery, her serious-minded husband, and their domestic felicity. It was a time of political upheaval on the Continent, and of growing agitation against the social conditions at home: a cause of uneasiness to the prosperous middle-class. In this uneasiness the Royal couple stood as a symbol of stability and order, both in national and home life. It was not surprising that the cult of home and children, springing as it did from a natural human impulse, should have been sentimentalized, often to absurdity, by an unconscious fear of social revolution.

The father was the unquestioned master of the home, in the sense that he alone had any legal standing. One does not believe that the majority of early Victorian husbands were autocratic despots, but the power they possessed under the law must have caused many a high-spirited wife to discipline

herself to unhappiness, rather than break up what had
turned out to be an unfortunate marriage. Apart from the
dread of losing her children, it would have taken a very
strong reason—unbearable treatment or neglect—to make
the average woman even contemplate leaving her husband.

She was the centre of the home, and she built her life
round her family. She had been trained to think of family
relationships in terms of duty as well as of love, and mixed
with her affection for her children there was something that
every one took for granted: the expectancy of filial obedience. This must have led to stresses and strains in family life
which we, in our day, have been taught to think of in
psychological terms. The early Victorian mother would have
considered such analysis outrageous. A certain amount of
dignity, formality, and courtesy were essential to the
accepted idea of home life, and arguments and disputes
between parents and children had no part in their ordered
existence.

The mother was no being who sat apart, demanding
deference and homage. True, in the wealthier households
the children were left in charge of nurses and governesses,
visits to the parental drawing-room being made an occasion;
but in the middle-class home the mother had her hand on all
the reins, especially those which concerned her children.

There is a belief that early Victorian women generally
left the management of their infants to incompetent nurses.
Many probably did, when servants of all kinds were so cheap
to employ. But the books on child-care, the "Answers to
Correspondents" in magazines, the editorials written by
physicians—all tend to show that large numbers of mothers
were genuinely anxious to learn about the nurture and up-
bringing of children. Perhaps they had begun to connect
the appalling infant mortality rate with the ignorant and
superstitious methods of midwives and untrained nurse-
maids.

The early history of the infant welfare movement shows
that there had for long been doctors who made persistent
efforts to educate mothers to their responsibilities. There
was published advice on the rearing of the young from the

eighteenth century onward; leaders and articles in various journals throughout the eighteen-thirties and -forties stressed the dangers of ignorance and the importance of understanding a child's needs.

A writer in the *Lancet* in 1851 was plain-spoken. In reviewing a book written by a physician especially for young mothers, *A Child's First Hour, with suggestions for some alterations in the Management of New-Born Infants*, he commented that it was:

"A most useful little book which should be in the hands of every mother, whether actual or in prospect. It is admirably calculated to banish for ever the mischievous practices of the self-opinionated tribe, of which Dickens's Mrs Gamp is no overdrawn portrait; and may suggest even to the accoucheur a thing or two which have not before occurred to his mind."

There is a slightly sinister note in an advertisement which appears in another newspaper.

"Dr Conquest's *Letters to a Mother* on the Management Of Herself and her Children in Health and Disease, with Remarks on the Use of Chloroform."

No restriction was put on the sale of chloroform or other drugs of that nature, and the quickest way to quieten a crying infant was to 'give him a little something soothing.' Many of the cordials and soothing syrups which had such a wide sale were mixtures of laudanum and treacle. If the directions were followed a child might be only doped, but with a careless or drunken nursemaid in charge the results could be more dire.

In the proper hands chloroform was taking a great deal of the terror from accidents and operations. Charles Greville was deeply impressed by its possibilities. In this extract from *The Greville Memoirs* (December 24, 1847) we get, incidentally, a glimpse of the medical etiquette of the time:

"I went yesterday to St George's Hospital to see the chloroform tried. A boy two and a half years old was cut for a stone. He was put to sleep in a minute . . . the operation lasted about twenty minutes. . . . The chloroform was

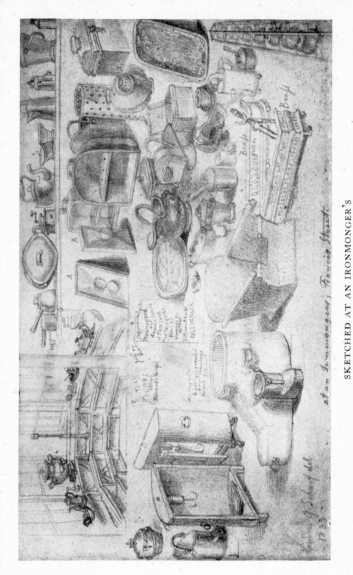

SKETCHED AT AN IRONMONGER'S

From a pencil drawing by G. Scharf

By courtesy of the Trustees of the British Museum

32

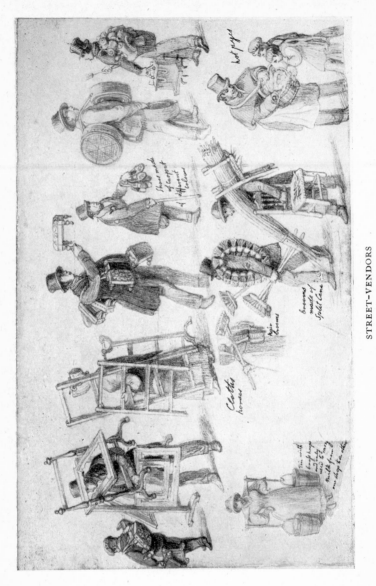

STREET-VENDORS

From a pencil drawing by G. Scharf

By courtesy of the Trustees of the British Museum

33

applied from time to time, and the child never exhibited the slightest sign of consciousness, and it was exactly the same as operating on a dead body. A curious example was shown of what is called the etiquette of the profession. The operator could not extract the stone, so at last he handed the instrument to Keate, who is the finest operator possible, and he got hold of the stone. . . . The first man begged to have the forceps back so that he might draw it out, and it was transferred to him; but in taking it he let go the stone, and the whole thing had to be done over again. It was accomplished, but not, of course, without increasing the local inflammation and endangering the life of the child. I asked Keate why, when he had got hold of the stone, he did not draw it out. He said the other man's 'dignity' would have been hurt if he had not been allowed to complete what he had begun!

"I have no words to express my admiration for this invention, which is the greatest blessing ever bestowed on mankind, and the inventor the greatest of benefactors, whose memory ought to be venerated by countless millions for ages to come."

For minor ailments the mistress of a household was expected to know the proper remedies and how to make them. In most cookery-books there was a section on home-made medicinal brews and salves, some of them age-old. A great many of these recipes contained herbs, which were grown in most gardens.

The apothecary was the doctor for the average middle-class family. A physician might be called in for serious illness, but the local Apothecary's Hall had pills and potions for most everyday complaints. A favourite nostrum was liquorice, another was castor-oil; and rubbing the chest with camphorated oil was the classic method of defeating a cough or cold.

The mother supervised the schoolroom as well as the nursery. She was usually responsible for the children's lessons until such time as they could benefit from a daily governess and visiting masters. Herself the product of a

C

Regency education which stressed accomplishments and manners and decried 'learning,' she naturally thought of the education of her daughters in the same terms. But she had a great respect for information, for masses of facts; and these she proceeded to drill into small heads by a system of questions and answers.

This ingenious form of mechanical instruction was perfected by a Miss Mangnall, a Yorkshire schoolmistress, whose textbook Mangnall's *Questions* (*Historical and Miscellaneous Questions for the Use of Young People*) was the standby in schoolrooms up and down the land. Most teaching books for the young followed this model, one of the most popular being *The Child's Guide to Knowledge*, "by a Lady" (Mrs R. Ward). It ran into over fifty editions, and here are several examples from its pages:

Q. What is sago?
A. The inner pith of a species of palm-tree growing in the Moluccas and Ceram.

Q. Where are these islands situated?
A. In Asia, between Australia and China.

Q. How is sago prepared for use?
A. The tree is sawn into pieces, and the pith taken out, and ground to a fine powder.

Q. What is then done with it?
A. It is rubbed through a fine hair sieve, mixed with water into a thick paste, and dried in a furnace.

Q. When were pins first used and made?
A. They were invented in France, in 1543, in the reign of Francis 1st; before this art was discovered, the ladies used small skewers made of wood, bone and ivory.

Q. What queen first made use of pins in England?
A. Catherine Howard, the fifth wife of Henry 8th.

Q. Were they not considered a great luxury, and not fit for common use?
A. Yes; the maker was not allowed to sell them in an open shop, except on two days of the year, at the beginning of January.

Q. What old custom did this give rise to?

A. To husbands giving their wives money at the beginning
of the year, to buy a few pins; therefore money allowed
to a wife for her own private spending is even now
called 'pin-money.'

There was no attempt to make a child think for himself;
everything was learnt by rote. Elementary 'summing,' the
use of the globes, and improving books which pointed a
moral were further lessons within a mother's compass.

She took especial pains in teaching her children manners
and social sense. In an age of growing decorum and formality it was necessary for children to understand polite behaviour at an early age. It was considered part of a child's
training to be able to speak clearly and well; and if, to our
ears, the stilted phrases, the rounded periods of conversation—even family conversation—sound artificial, we must
keep in mind the formality of domestic life and the tacit insis-
tence on personal and mutual respect.

So the mother passed on, as adequately as she could, the
kind of education which she had had herself. There were,
however, new ideas in education filtering through. From
time to time news appeared of the work of Froebel and
others in Switzerland and Germany, pioneers of a new kind
of teaching for small children, based on the principles of
natural development. Travellers brought back accounts of
Froebel's kindergarten schools, and his death in 1852 was
taken as an opportunity by educationists to describe his
achievements and press for his new kind of school to be
established in England.

But it takes many years for revolutionary ideas in education to take root. The early Victorian mother, with Mangnall's *Questions* or *The Child's Guide* before her, continued to
teach her children by rote; and the same method was fol
lowed by governesses and those who kept boarding
schools.

The mother of a family led a busy life, but her time was
not entirely filled with domestic tasks and social duties.
Home recreation played a very important part in family life,
and several hours a day were kept free for relaxation.

I cannot think why it is so taken for granted that the Victorian family led a dull life. The early Victorians belonged to an age when it was natural to find plenty of amusement at home; the books of games which survive, the diaries and letters giving long accounts of family entertainments, do not indicate dullness or boredom.

The Girl's Own Book, published in 1848, gives over a hundred and thirty games to be played at home: garden games, parlour games, charades and rebuses, as well as team games in which parents and children of all ages could join. They may seem unsophisticated to twentieth-century eyes, but they also had something which was largely to disappear later —zest and a sense of fun.

Children were taught chess and draughts at an early age; and they played dominoes, loto, and counting games with an ivory ball and cup. Battledore and shuttlecock in the garden in summer, or over the dining-room table in winter, was a family favourite; and there was a vogue for balancing games, in which ivory or polished-wood shapes had to be kept balanced on a cord stretched between two sticks.

Besides games there were table peep-shows—long frames enclosed in paper, with pictures or many-coloured kaleidoscopes at one end, and a magnifying eyepiece at the other. Children collected peepshows, cutting out and painting the tiny scenes, and giving periodical entertainments to their friends.

Another source of pleasure was automaton dolls—small models of the life-size automata which were exhibited regularly in London and the big cities. These little figures were constructed round clockwork machinery, and were very ingenious. There was the chess-player, "an image dressed like a Turk, who sat at a board and played as good a game of chess as if he had brains in his wooden skull." There was the Spanish Lancer, who caught a cap on the point of his sword without stopping his horse, a toy circus with a fountain playing in the centre, and singing-birds, acrobats, jugglers, dancing-dolls. All were well and accurately made; young eyes were trained to appreciate good workmanship.

Miniature representations of grand events were among other juvenile playthings; so were toy theatres:

"They showed her a representation of the grand procession of the King of England, printed on a long narrow roll of paper pasted on silk, which paper was unwound like a riband-yard from a Tunbridge-ware box, and it could be screwed up again after being sufficiently seen. It was many yards in length, the figures were elegantly designed and beautifully coloured.

"They had, also, a little theatre, with a great number of scenes, and a variety of very small dolls, dressed in appropriate habits to personate the actors.

"Then there was a portable diorama, containing twelve coloured views of castles, abbeys, temples and mountain scenery. Each of these little landscapes was fixed in turn as the back-scene of a sort of miniature stage. The skies and lights of these views were all transparent, and there were other skies which turned on rollers, and represented sunrise, moonlight, sunshine and thunder-clouds. These second skies being placed behind those of the picture, were slowly unrolled by turning a small handle, and produced the most varied and beautiful effects on the scenery, which could thus at pleasure be illuminated gradually with sunshine or moonbeams, or darkened with the clouds of a gathering storm."[1]

The 'little theatre' was perhaps the greatest favourite of all in the early Victorian family. Toy theatres had been a popular home amusement since the beginning of the century, and by the thirties there were many refinements available; besides the sheets of characters which could be bought for a few pence there were tin oil-containers for footlights, and chemical powders which gave out coloured fire when lit—red for a conflagration, blue for scenes of mystery.

The whole family took part in toy-theatre performances. First the girls coloured the characters, then the boys pasted these on cardboard and cut them out, fixing them in the tin or wooden slides which were pushed on to the little stage from the wings. Papa helped with the construction of the scenery and the framework of the proscenium arch;

[1] From an account of the entertainment of a country child by her town cousins.

Mama assisted with the sewing of the curtains which boxed in the table-stage.

The plays were abridged versions of successes in the adult theatre: *Black-Eyed Susan*, *Jack Sheppard*, and the classic *Miller and His Men*—plays with plenty of blood and thunder. The cardboard players were manipulated by the children, hidden behind the curtains or screens, while parents, servants, relations, and neighbours sat in front, an admiring audience.

III

HOUSES

THE terraces, crescents, and squares of late eighteenth-century houses which are found in London and in many country and seaside towns give us an idea of the kind of home in which the middle class lived during the first years of Victoria's reign. The houses are tall and narrow, with pleasant lines and well-proportioned rooms. The front doors have fanlights, and where there is decoration on the surrounds it is discreet and in keeping.

The houses built in the thirties followed, in the main, the lines of Georgian and Regency architecture. Change began to come in the forties. The wealthy merchants and factory-owners wanted something to show for their money. Houses became larger, more imposing, with pillared porticos and stucco façades. The craftsman-builder, trained in former days to relate his design to its surroundings and allow it to have some individuality, began to give place to the speculative firm which bought up the woods and open land on the edges of the existing residential areas. This advertisement from the *Illustrated London News* in 1843 is typical of many:

"Westbourne Terrace: to be Let or Sold; an excellent Family House, fitted up regardless of expense, with coach-house, stabling . . . etc. This terrace being half a mile in length, and 40 feet wider than Portland Place, will, when completed, be the most splendid in the Metropolis. Its superior salubrity is also unquestionable, the soil being gravel and the ground floor of the house 70 feet above high-water mark, and on a level with the attics of Eaton and Belgrave Squares. Several first-class mansions, now in carcase, may be completed according to the taste of the purchaser or tenant, for a fixed sum. Houses of a similar class in the Villa style, are also in the course of erection in the Gloucester Road . . . and will be ready for occupation in the Spring. . . ."

The "villa style" grew increasingly popular. It lent itself to the neo-Gothic ideas then becoming fashionable; the red-brick, gabled house with its semi-circular sweep of lawn or shrubbery in front was soon to be the hall-mark of 'comfortable circumstances.' The cheap builders followed the new style, and rows of ugly little houses in red or yellow brick began to cover the land behind the bigger houses.

It is these which we generally call 'Victorian,' but the family house of the thirties and forties was still part of the Georgian or Regency inheritance, as can be seen from the topographical drawings of the period.

Furniture was also comparatively simple. It was not until later that massive mahogany sideboards and ball-fringed hangings came in. The Catalogue of the Great Exhibition shows examples of the debasement of taste which followed the rise of money without breeding to guide it—the heavy tables and chairs, the elaborate fixtures of gilt and iron, the emphasis on florid decoration. Until that date furniture and fittings retained something of the elegance and simplicity of the Regency period. In the forties there was still a tradition of handmade furniture; numerous cabinet-makers' shops, with ornamental frontage carved to show the craftsman's skill, were to be found in every town.

But the machine age had come by the fifties, and most furniture was mass-produced and cheap:

"THOSE ABOUT TO MARRY should obtain the improved book of estimates . . . where they will find a four-roomed cottage can be completely furnished for 23 guineas; a six-roomed house completely and neatly for £70; an eight-roomed house, with many elegancies and substantialities for £140; and a mansion of fourteen rooms furnished with that style, beauty and durability for which this house has obtained so large a share of public patronage, for 350 guineas. A single room or single article at the same moderate charge. Smith's Warerooms, next door to the Clerkenwell Police Court.''[1]

Furniture was generally made of rosewood or mahogany. Four-poster beds were still usual, as one can see from the illustrations in the first editions of Dickens's novels. Brass and iron bedsteads began to come in during the forties, and were very fashionable. Feather-bed mattresses were invariable, and the top cover of the bed was usually a quilt, or a thick damask spread.

Bedrooms were cold in winter. The warming-pans which nowadays adorn so many 'olde tea shoppes' had a real purpose in Victorian days. Filled with hot coals, they were slowly circulated inside the bed before the inmate climbed in. Rubber hot-water bottles were unknown, though rubber was used in other ways—for 'galoshes' and capes, and also in the manufacture of collapsible boats, which were to reappear more than a century later as air-sea-rescue dinghies.

Victorian bathrooms were not unknown, but they were rare. In most houses hot water was taken up to the bedrooms and poured into a tin hip-bath; and, of course, it had to be taken down to the kitchen again after it had been used.

The living-rooms were warmed by great coal fires; coal was very cheap, as was the labour to fetch and carry it. If the master of the house were of a modern turn of mind a many-branched gasolier would spout bright fans of blue-yellow flame in the main rooms. Most houses, however, were still lighted by oil-lamps and candles. In the thirties and forties colza-oil was used—oil made from rape-seeds. Later, paraffin-oil gave better results. In large houses there was a lamp-room, where the many lamps needed throughout the house were cleaned and kept, and where the moulds for making candles were stored.

Lamplight and candlelight: these are typical of the evening scene in the early Victorian household, the warm glow

[1] *Illustrated London News.*

throwing up the background of striped wallpaper and bro-
cade curtains.

Towards the middle of the century this interior began
to have a heavier, richer look. There were more pictures on
the walls—engravings of pastoral scenes, water-colours
painted by the ladies of the family, portraits in crayons or
oils. Professional artists flourished; before the day of the
photograph it was usual to have members of the family
sketched or painted.

The coming of the photograph caused great enthusiasm
and excitement. Daguerre and others had been working on
the new discovery since the eighteen-twenties, and by the
forties there were photographers ready to supply this new
form of family picture. In 1846 Mr Claudet was advertising:

"Claudet's Daguerrotype portraits lately so much eulo-
gised by the leading papers . . . are all non-inverted, and
when coloured by Mr Manson, an artist of ability, are the
most exquisite miniatures. Mr Claudet operates himself, and
never allows an inferior portrait to leave his establishment.
Ladies have the attendance of a respectable female. Open
from 9 o'clock at 18 King William Street."

But photographs were an expensive novelty for the average family, and the Victorian album familiar to us usually
dates from the sixties.

Below stairs the early Victorian house was dark, cold,
comfortless. The housewife might well put on an extra
shawl as she descended from her living-rooms to the basement to unlock the store-cupboards and see that all was in
order. Stone floors and slate shelves in larders and sculleries
were icy to the touch. Only the kitchen was warm, heated
by a large kitchen range which ate up coal and needed constant attention. In summer the kitchen was like a furnace,
for all the cooking was done on the range. Gas, though used
for lighting, was not yet provided for cooking; the first gas-
cooker was exhibited in 1851, but cookers were not fitted
in private houses for a number of years after that date.

Kitchen utensils were solid and good. Pans were made of
iron and tinned copper; some saucepans had a china lining

for double boiling. On the kitchen wall hung a burnished row of dish-covers, indispensible in an age when all the food was carried from an underground kitchen to the dining-room upstairs. Pestle and mortar for pounding sugar stood on a shelf, together with the sugar-clippers; sugar was sold in cones, and had to be clipped and pounded. The house-wife generally did this herself, as sugar was an expensive commodity and had to be kept locked away.

In summer the basements of houses became exceedingly unpleasant because of defective sanitation. Plumbing was still in a primitive state. Water was piped to many houses in the towns, but more often it had to be pumped from a well in the yard. In times of drought extra water had to be bought from the water-carts which came round. Only the sanitary authorities seemed interested in the source of their supply.

Water-closets, or 'necessaries,' as they were known to the polite, had been fitted in some of the big houses since the eighteenth century, and from the eighteen-thirties onward they began to come into more general use. But in most dwellings the outside privy in garden or yard was usual. There was no main drainage. Cesspools were dug to take the sewage, and these were sometimes left unemptied and new ones made. Glazed sewage pipes were introduced in the early forties; they were an improvement on the flat-bottomed pipes used before, but even they were not effective, the glaze cracking and the pipes becoming porous.

The foul conditions which resulted were as common in the fashionable houses as they were in the slums and rook-eries which seamed the streets behind the mansions. The average Victorian parent saw no connexion between the leaky sewage pipes beneath his house and the illness which played such a disturbingly large part in his family life. There were outbreaks of cholera, like the terrible epidemics which swept the land in the forties; but at all times there was a danger of fever.

The doctors, and the public-spirited men who urged sanitary reform, knew well enough where the danger lay. After a long struggle against prejudice and apathy the first Public Health Act was passed in 1848; and the consequent

improved sanitary methods caused a fall in the death-rate
within a few years. But all this took time, and in the family
of the forties and fifties the loss of a parent, brother, or sister
from fever was an ever-present possibility—an act of Providence, as they thought.

In the country, houses were larger than in town; land was
cheap, and a man with a moderate income could enjoy a
home in which there was plenty of room, a good garden,
a paddock, and an orchard. There would be several store-
rooms and a still-room, for the housewife gathered her own
fruit in summer, and made it into preserves, and wines.

Many country houses, even small ones, had their own
ice-store. The many iced puddings, sweets, and drinks
which the Victorian housewife served—a century before the
days of domestic refrigerators—were made possible by the
storing of ice in small ice-houses, which were dug like a well
in the garden and lined with brick. In winter ice was taken
off the ponds and cut up into blocks which were wrapped in
thick layers of straw and packed into the ice-house. Close-
fitting double doors effectively insulated the store, in which
the ice kept in excellent condition.

In country and town, then, the middle-class background
gives an impression of ease and comfort, without the osten-
tation which was to characterize the later decades of Victoria's reign. It is this very comfort which throws into dark
relief the other side of the picture:

"The Royal Palace in St James's Park has for its background the reeking sinks of Pimlico. The gorgeous silk-
shops of Regent Street depend for their supply on the
poverty-stricken hovels of Spitalfields. You cannot judge
of London by the sight of its gayer thoroughfares. Turn
aside at any point, and you will find that behind the smiling
front of wealth and splendour, there swarm hordes of
miserable people, immured in close streets into which the
sun never peeps."[1]

"In the villages, the cattle on most farms are better
housed than the agricultural labourers and their families.
Foxhounds live in luxury compared with them. Look into

[1] Henry Mayhew, *London Labour and the London Poor* (1851), Vol. I.

the peasants' cottage in any county—in the richest agricultural counties—and what do you find? A mud floor uneven and damp. A hole in the wall serves as window. Around the doors are puddles, fed from the steaming stye of pigs. . . . In the one apartment which constitutes the whole of the peasant's house the parents, with their sons and daughters of all ages, live, eat, wash, and sleep. Numbers die annually of fever, which is caused partly by the unwholesomeness of their habitations and partly by the filthiness of the water they drink. We have obtained a Health of Towns Bill, but a Health of Rural Districts Bill seems quite as imperatively called for."[1]

In town and country the tale was the same; the housing provided for the labouring poor was cheap, shoddy, and insanitary. Jerry-builders bought up undrained land, which was without a market value for anything else, and crowded on to it as many dwellings as they could. These were built without foundations and with few windows; the window-tax was not repealed until 1851. There was no sanitation inside the houses; a privy and pump or tap were provided at the end of each 'court' and often had to serve fifty or sixty families.

In the expanding industrial towns of the North the same type of jerry-builder put up blocks of tenements, some of which remain to this day, a heritage of slums. In the Midlands acres of back-to-back dwellings surrounded the factories; these back-to-backs had not even room for a yard in which the housewife could hang out her washing. Perhaps the worst of all were the cellar-dwellings, common in London and other big cities. It was a heartbreaking task for a woman to make a decent home in such conditions.

A never-ending battle went on throughout the thirties and forties—the reformers against the landlords and property-owners, who saw no reason for making improvements. But the constant outbreaks of disease in these fetid courts pointed to perpetual danger, and men like Edwin Chadwick, Lyon Playfair, Southwood Smith, and others worked hard to collect evidence and to impress upon official quarters the necessity for action.

[1] From an article in *Eliza Cook's Journal* in the late forties.

Chadwick was a barrister, and one of the ablest of the nineteenth-century reformers. He was associated with most of the progressive movements of his day, but will be chiefly remembered for his work in sanitation. As one of the commissioners appointed to investigate factory labour and the Poor Laws, he found that large numbers of labouring people died prematurely from consumption, cholera, and other pestilential fevers. He directed a far-reaching inquiry to find the reason for this abnormally high death-rate, and published the *Report on the Health of Towns*, in 1842. A contemporary review of this Report says: "Such a revelation of the horrors lying concealed beneath the fair surface of our modern Christian civilization has never been made before."

The horrors included evidence of foul water sold for drinking purposes, and of defective drainage everywhere. In some places sewage contaminated the actual water-supply. Chadwick's Report suggested many reforms, the principal ones being the provision of a municipal water-supply, efficient drainage, a public health service, and a national burial service.

The Report created opposition from those who thought reforms were an unnecessary waste of money, but public opinion was stirred. There were many people in that age of wealth who could not tolerate the idea of subhuman standards of life among their fellow-men, and Chadwick and his friends found supporters. The setting up of the first General Board of Health in 1848 was the direct result of Chadwick's labours; it was the beginning of official recognition that public health was the nation's concern.

The Board was established, but there were no appreciable results for a long time. Powers were given to local authorities—permissive powers, not directives. A local authority could reform its sanitary system if it wished; it was not bound to do so. The results were not unexpected. Vigorous, public-spirited local councils did what they could to make improvements, others did nothing. In 1852, four years after the setting up of the Board, Samuel Smiles was attacking the builders of new slums in *Eliza Cook's Journal*:

"Wholesome dwellings cost no more than unwholesome

ones. . . . Homes should be built on ground which has
been thoroughly well drained . . . and the streets efficiently
paved and sewered. . . . No working-man with a family
should be satisfied with fewer than two sleeping-rooms, and
many ought not to have less than three."

The problem engaged the interest of some one on the
highest level—the Prince Consort. He was the Patron of
the Society for Improving the Dwellings of the Industrial
Classes, and much good work was done by this body. The
Prince himself designed a model block of houses which was
built near the Great Exhibition. It was, indeed, a model of
good housing compared with the hovels in which most
workmen of the time lived. There were four self-contained
dwellings in the block, each containing a living-room, three
sleeping-apartments, a kitchen, a water-closet, and a lobby;
the water-supply was carefully sited, and there were plenty
of cupboards and shelves.

One would like to be able to record that the Prince's
model tenement was taken up with enthusiasm, but the
Royal lead was not followed. Whatever influence the Prince
Consort had in "improving the dwellings of the industrial
classes" was cut short by his death. There is little doubt
that, had he lived, he would greatly have encouraged the
men who were trying to better the terrible living-conditions
of the poor.

The working-class housewife had grim surroundings, but
she made attempts to keep her home and children clean.
This was an undertaking, when every pint of water had to
be carried from the common pump or tap, and before the
days of municipal wash-houses. The establishment of these
washhouses was actually due to a working-woman, an Irish
immigrant. Here is the story from *Baths and Wash Houses:
the History of their Rise and Progress*, by G. A. Cape (1854):

"When the cholera was raging Catherine Wilkinson, a
poor woman who lived in one of the back-streets of Liverpool, knowing from experience the misery and unhealthi-
ness that is always consequent upon dirt, and the discomfort
arising from washing in confined rooms, and possessing,
moreover, a copper in her own kitchen, hit upon the plan

of serving her neighbours. . . . She offered to those who wished it the opportunity of washing at her copper; this boon, small as it may appear, was eagerly sought. In a short time her yard, her kitchen, and her passage were crowded by those who had not this accommodation at home."

Mrs Wilkinson was aided by some charitable persons, and for some time eighty-five families used this humble wash-house. "From this simple circumstance," Cape goes on, "the idea of erecting public baths and wash-houses was taken." The first was built at Liverpool in 1842; a penny was charged for a tub of water for washing clothes. By 1850 London and many of the provincial cities had built baths and washhouses, and some also had swimming-baths. The establishment at Lambeth offered an extra facility—an infant-school and nursery where women could leave their children while doing their washing.

Full advantage was taken of the new washing- and bathing-places wherever they were provided; more people used them every year. There were letters to the Press prophesying that the new municipal facilities would be abused—the period's equivalent to our 'coals in the bath' forebodings. But the idea spread from town to town; in the course of a few years there was a system of public washhouses throughout the country. And it had all developed from the neighbourly kindness of a woman in a back-street. Her features are commemorated in the staircase window of the Lady Chapel in Liverpool Cathedral—"a poor helper of the poor."

THE STRAND, LONDON, FROM THE CORNER OF VILLIERS STREET

From a water-colour drawing by G. Scharf

[P. 54]

48

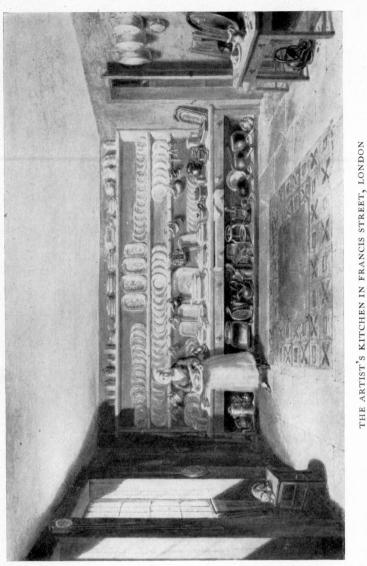

THE ARTIST'S KITCHEN IN FRANCIS STREET, LONDON

From a water-colour drawing by G. Scharf

By courtesy of the Trustees of the British Museum

49

IV

SERVANTS

The Typical Servant—"Nelly Armstrong"—Mrs Carlisle's Servants—
Wages—Beer-money—Upper-class Establishments—Middle-class Mistresses
—Mothering Sunday Custom

A<small>N</small> article in *Eliza Cook's Journal* for January 1854 begins:

"Domestic service is a subject in which every middle and upper-class family in England is interested . . . for the entire comfort of the home depends in a greater or lesser degree upon the cleanliness, honesty, sobriety, attention, and industry of those who serve in it."

The Victorian housewife who read that sentence when it was first published must have sighed, for though domestic servants were easy to get and wages were low, the treasure who could be counted upon for cleanliness, honesty, and sobriety was hard to find, unless she was a young girl fresh from the country, who had not yet been hardened by a frequent change of situation.

Mary, the housemaid at Mr Nupkins', of Ipswich—Mary of the cherry-coloured ribbons who took the fancy of Sam Weller—is the idealized servant-maid of early Victorian times. Then there is Miss Matty's Martha, plain, blunt-tongued, loyal, whom we love afresh every time we open *Cranford*. But these two are by no means typical of the early Victorian servant.

Her background was nearly always the same: one of extreme poverty. If she came from the country she had probably been sent out from a labourer's cottage where it was no longer possible to feed or clothe her. She had either to go into a factory or into service, and anxious parents may have

D

decided that she would be safer, and more sure of food and shelter, in a good 'place.' If—as was more probable—she came from the wretched slums which formed what the brothers Mayhew called the "jungle of London," she could not be expected to know the ordinary habits of civilized life, let alone refinements like cleanliness, honesty, and sobriety.

The Victorian housewife who engaged a servant always took on a responsibility. If she were a good mistress she could sometimes turn unpromising material into a faithful, industrious member of the household, one who had her own niche in the life of the family. An overbearing or tyrannical mistress could drive a girl to desperation.

In the article already quoted above the writer goes on to examine the relations between mistress and servant:

"It will be admitted that a large proportion of the young women who go out to service are very ignorant, that many of them have been badly brought up. The greater, how-ever, is it the duty of the mistress to make up for the deficiencies of such young women's early training. We fear that mistresses generally expect qualifications on the part of their servants too nearly approaching perfection. For £10 they expect a young woman to have the self-denial of an anchorite, the method of a philosopher, the skill of a Soyer, and the industry of a steam-engine.

"It becomes a mistress who is considerate and charitable to be forbearant of the weakness of servants, so many of whom have been unfavourably circumstanced in their early years. Were mistresses to act in such a spirit, great indeed is the crime and misery that would be saved."

This last was undoubtedly true. Servants were often dismissed without notice and without a 'character.' Those who came from far country places were often unable to return home; others who had been obtained from orphanages and charity schools had no homes, and were forced to take refuge with anyone who would befriend them.

Nelly Armstrong, a novel published in 1853, traces the downward career of a servant-girl who has been dismissed without good reason. At the end the author admonishes the thoughtless mistress:

"And this, Madam, is your work! Yet you are a woman highly esteemed in society; mothers quote you to their daughters as a model of propriety . . . of active benevolence. Year after year, with comfortable self-approval, you behold your name enrolled among other subscribers to Magdalene Asylums and shelters for the outcast and profligate. Woman! little do you dream of having been instrumental in fashioning an asylum for them. You did not anticipate the consequence, I grant you, when you turned your servant from your door, without doing her the justice of listening to her trembling explanations, but it is as truly yours as if you had planned it."

Even so valued a servant as Wilson, Elizabeth Barrett's maid, would have been treated with the same lack of humanity. Writing to Browning, when planning their elopement, Elizabeth Barrett says that she must take Wilson. "If I left her behind she would be turned into the street before sunset. Would it be right and just of me to permit it?" She knew her father would dismiss Wilson instantly for her part in the elopement.

Jane Welsh Carlyle's *Letters* give many vivid sketches of servants. One of the earliest of her domestics was Helen Mitchell, "Kircaldy Helen, one of the notabilities, and also the blessings, of our existence here," as Carlyle described her. Mrs Carlyle's feelings of responsibility towards her servants are well brought out in a letter to her mother-in-law in 1840:

"At present, I have got rather a heavy burden on my shoulders, the guarding of a human being from her perdition of strong liquors. My poor little Helen had been gradually getting more and more into the habit of tippling, until, some fortnight ago, she rushed down into a fit of the most decided drunkenness that I ever dreamed to witness. . . . Next day she looked black with shame and despair, and the next following, overcome by her tears and promises and self-upbraidings, I forgave her again, very much to my own surprise."

Mrs Carlyle forgave Kirkaldy Helen many times during the eleven years the girl served her in Cheyne Row. In spite of a genuine attachment to her mistress, Helen eventually came to a sad end through drink. She had many successors, good and bad; their comings and goings run like a knotted thread through the *Letters*.

Mrs Carlyle paid her servant "Twelve pounds a year and one-pound-ten for beer-money, which she may drink or save as she likes." Twelve pounds a year was a good wage; the average was eight or nine pounds, "with tea and sugar," and, of course, beer. Beer is constantly mentioned as an addition to servants' wages; it was a great deal cheaper than tea. The temperance societies began to agitate against the provision of beer, insisting that it was the surest way of starting young girls on the path to chronic drunkenness; and in time they were able to have beer-money substituted. This led to a slight increase in the general level of wages, but the habit of beer-drinking among servants persisted.

The housewife got her servants through the local tradesmen as a rule; there were no established registries until later in the century. Another source was the orphanage or the workhouse. Philanthropic people supported institutions where young women could safely stay between situations. A handbook for Richmond, in Surrey, advertised:

"INFANT NURSERY AND SERVANTS' HOME. To provide for the care of Infants during the absence of their Mothers while engaged in work away from home. It also affords a Home and Useful Occupation for girls too young for service or temporarily out of employ."

In the large establishments of the nobility and landed gentry there was a hierarchy of the servants' hall, with menservants on the higher levels, and distinct grades lower down, reaching from the housekeeper to the scullery-maid. Any volume of *Punch* throughout the early Victorian period has a dozen or more cartoons satirizing the snobbery and pretensions of upper servants, and the servility of those who waited on them. The prevailing caste feeling of the period was quickly picked up by servants in important families, and a strict code of precedence was kept up at meals in the servants' hall and in the procession to church on Sundays.

In the middle-class families a much more personal interest

was taken in the housemaid or cook. Her hours were very long: from six in the morning until the family retired at night. She might get a half-day every other Sunday, and several hours of freedom during the week—it depended on the mistress. In country districts it was a recognized thing to let the maids go out when the Fair came. A passage in a private diary dated 1848 indicates that one family was unusually broad-minded on other holiday occasions:

"It being race-time, Mary and Ellen attired themselves in their new shawls and bonnets and went to Epsom, so Mama and I prepared dinner. Mama adjured them to make no rough acquaintances."

The chief holiday for servants in country districts was Mothering Sunday. This was in mid-Lent, and it was traditional to allow a girl to go home and spend that day with her mother. The mistress baked a large, rich fruit cake for the girl to take home as a gift; this was probably the origin of the simnel-cake. The cake itself was boiled in a cloth before being packed into a case of *simila*—fine white flour—and then well baked. It was said that some of these cakes were so solid that a girl could sit on the package on her journey home.

It was a pleasant custom, this simnel-giving, and rarely omitted, for it brought the mistress good luck:

> I'll thee a simnel bring
> 'Gainst thou go a-mothering,
> So that when she blesses thee
> Half that blessing thou'lt give to me.

V

SHOPS

THERE is in the Print Room of the British Museum a coloured drawing, by George Scharf, of the Strand as it was a hundred years ago. It is a picture which conveys the essence, the living atmosphere, of the shops where the early Victorian woman spent leisurely hours.

They have character, these shops. Small, beautifully proportioned, no two alike, they yet conform to a style which gives a satisfying sense of unity. The shop-windows are divided into panes, and are bow-fronted; there is an air of spaciousness about them, for all their apparent smallness.

Here are the Grocer and Tea-Man, and his neighbours the Saddler and the Oyster Warehouse, where Continental delicacies were to be had. The shops curve out of the picture into a Strand full of colour, the painted name-boards picked out in gold, the glazing bars of the windows painted or polished, the fasciæ ornamented with curly lettering.

Scharf was much interested in the everyday life of London, for there are dozens of his coloured drawings of streets, houses, and shops. There are all kinds of details: the inside of a hardware shop, with coal-scuttles and fire-irons, and of all things—a pressure-cooker. There is a charming drawing of a dairy, with two or three cows in a pen in one corner, and a dairyman with cans, a window piled with eggs, and a customer at the counter between the eggs and the cows. Scharf has written a note under the picture: "This I drew in Golden Lane in the City, in order to compare it with an elegant Milk Shop in the Quadrant, Piccadilly." Below is a drawing of the milk-shop under the colonnade of fashionable Piccadilly, but it is very ordinary compared with the Golden Lane dairy and its cows.

Besides the leisure which the early Victorian woman had for shopping, she went out knowing that she could buy anything she desired. The world sent its wares to the London shops: silks and spices from the East, teas from China and India, wool from Kashmir. Even if she were only 'middling comfortably off,' she could afford a reasonably good stand-ard in clothes and food, for there was a wide variety of every-thing.

It was the heyday of the individual shopkeeper, the man who owned his business and worked in it himself. He might be a craftsman, like a bootmaker, or a tradesman, like a linen-draper, but he knew his craft or his trade, and he also knew that *quality* counted.

There were as yet no department stores. A Mr Harrod, a tea-merchant, had taken over a small grocery business in the rather shabby residential district of Knightsbridge. A Mr Peter Robinson had a draper's shop in Oxford Street, oppo-site Jay's Mourning Warehouse. In the Tottenham Court Road, where there were still houses and gardens, Mr Maple was doing well with his furniture shop, and Mrs Heal was carrying on her late husband's business and making it prosper. Anything larger than a double-fronted shop was unusual.

The wealthy woman went shopping in her carriage; the middle-class woman took a cab or walked. The centre of London was still largely residential, and on a fine day it was pleasant to stroll along from one's house to Regent Street or Piccadilly, and gaze at the well-filled shop-windows.

Here was the silk-mercer's, festooned with the newest materials; flowered brocades made by the Spitalfields weavers, and sarsanet—that fine woven silk which looked so well on one's daughters. The shopping woman had no need to calculate how much material she would need, for she could buy a complete dress-length, anything from fifteen to twenty yards, according to the number of flounced over-skirts she had decided to have.

The laceman and embroiderer would not be far away. Besides selling hand-made lace this tradesman also had ribands, and ribands were important when dozens of yards were used on a gown—in ruchings and rouleaux, in edgings and cockades, in double and triple bows on sleeves and smoothly moulded bodices. There were embroidered ribands and taffeta-striped ribands, some with velvet spots and others with plush patterns—perfectly woven ribands, many of which survive to this day.

Now came the bonnet-shop, the window dressed with taste and a knowledge of what would catch the feminine eye; here one could buy lace and muslin caps for house wear, as well as bonnets. Past the glove-shop, with its array of hand-sewn English gloves, fine French gloves, and lace mittens; past the apothecary's, his windows glittering with great bottles of blue, green, and red waters, his Delft drug-jars framing the bow-window; past the china warehouse, with plates and cups stacked outside in a pyramid; and now down a side-street to pay an important visit.

Here is how a contemporary describes this discreetly tucked-away place:

"Through the wide sash windows I could see women's stays stretched on a line. Above the window was a framed and glazed sign: *Ann Gussett, Staymaker—Stays Wholesale or for Exportation*. Inside were some five-and-twenty women and girls busy in all operations of the trade, and apprentices boring holes in the stay-backs and fastening in bones, the journeywomen cutting out the strong twill foundations."

Back in the main street a shawl-shop caught the eye, its windows a rich medley of colours. There were silk shawls from France and the finest shawls of woven wool from India, so soft, they could be drawn through a wedding-ring. A large trade in imitation cashmere, made in the Midlands, developed in the forties, but it did not harm the India trade: the discriminating shopper knew the real thing when she saw it.

She may have lingered in the shawl-shop, expecting her husband to meet her here on his way home from the City; for he, too, had his purchases to make. If he came on horseback there were livery stables behind the shops where he could put up his horse for an hour or two, or he might patronize the omnibus, which came along at regular intervals. Or, of course, he could take a hansom-cab—not at all a proper vehicle for ladies, but popular with the gentlemen.

There was plenty to attract masculine attention in those bow-fronted windows. The booksellers', the print-shops, the whip-maker's, the hatter's, the little corner shop which advertised above its portal, in flowing script, *Snuff and Segars*—all were set out for the prosperous Victorian gentleman.

Husband and wife might stop at yet another shop on their way home. Here was a choice of sweetmeats for the children. The window was bright with many colours—saucers of almond rock, brandy-balls, sugar-plums and acid-drops; trays of hard-bake and candied almonds; peppermint-cakes and crystallized leaves. There were sweetmeats with names to match their exotic hues: elecampane, a candy flavoured with the herb of that name; and Nelson's Buttons, a peppermint confection stamped and shaped to the semblance of a naval button; and Buonaparte's Ribs—though what they were I cannot tell, save that they were much disapproved of by one old lady who records their "taking away the appetite for a good mutton dinner."

Besides the shops there were street-vendors of all kinds trying to attract the attention of the housewife. Baskets, brooms, brushes, and clothes-horses were made at home and hawked round the streets by men and women carrying their wares on their heads or festooned round them on frames. Fruit and vegetables were sold from large baskets carried on the arm, sometimes from panniers which weighed down a mournfully walking donkey.

Bread and milk could also be bought in the streets. The baker, dressed in white, went slowly along, calling: "Hot loaves! Hot loaves!" while a small assistant trundled a cart piled high with bread. There was more sale for this at the small houses in the back-streets than at the residences in the squares and terraces; the middle-class housewife baked her bread at home. The commercial bakeries, not yet under supervision from the public health authorities, were often cellars where the bakers worked in filthy conditions, sleeping beside their kneading-troughs and ovens. It was difficult to keep vermin and flour-pests under control in these underground bakeries, which sent out fevers as well as hot loaves with their white-clad bread-sellers.

Milk could be bought at dairies such as Scharf has pictured, but it was often brought round by milkmaids, strong country girls who carried wooden pails supported by a yoke across the shoulders. Some of the milk came in from the countryside surrounding the big towns, but cows were actually kept in the towns themselves. In London there were cowkeepers in Mile End, Tottenham, the Edgware Road, Westminster, Paddington, and many other districts. Cows were also kept in stalls under the arches of Cannon Street and other railway stations; they were brought there from the country after having calved, were fed on brewers' grain, and kept for milking until they could give no more. They were then sold to the butchers, and replaced by fresh cows.

The street-hawkers appeared in the early mornings, and their cries could be heard at intervals throughout the day, to die away as darkness came on and their wares could no longer be seen. But darkness made no difference to the shops, summer or winter. They remained open until there appeared to be no probability of further custom; then they were reluctantly closed.

Looking back, it seems to us that the shops of a hundred years ago were open during all a man's waking hours, except on Sundays. There was no legislation to regulate the hours of shop-assistants. A tradesman knew that he would have to work long and hard in that age of plenty: competition was fierce. The surest way of attracting customers was to be always at their service. The shopkeeper

was willing to put in twelve or fourteen hours a day, and
he expected his assistants to do the same—and to remain
smiling and at attention if a customer came in at a late hour
and took her time. The slogan "The customer is always
right" had not been invented—the Victorians did not have
slogans. But that principle was nevertheless the foundation
of shopkeeping.

The eagerness of the tradesman to please could turn a
woman into a thoughtless bully. She would ask for a small
purchase to be sent to her house when she could easily have
carried it, and counter-men often had to do a weary round
of deliveries after the shop had at last closed. The mid-
century commissions appointed to inquire into the condition
of shop-assistants all brought to light this form of exploitation.

Once the facts became known public opinion began to
make itself felt. There were sermons on the subject: "Op-
pressive Shop Labour," preached by the Rev. James Ralph,
and "Christian Labour, not Egyptian Bondage," preached
by the Rev. Mr Stoughton, both afterwards published as
pamphlets.

Public interest was also growing in the new Early Closing
Movement. In 1842 the "Metropolitan Drapers' Association for Abridging the Hours of Business of All Trades"
had been formed, and the Early Closing Movement developed from this association. Its aim was to persuade
employers to agree to reasonable hours for their assistants.
A substantial number of shopkeepers and warehouse-
owners did in fact begin to shorten the hours of their
employees—and advertised the fact in their local newspapers.

The radical journals of the day felt that it was also
necessary to educate the shopping woman, and there were
editorials and articles in their columns appealing to her
sympathy and common sense. Pamphlets and books were
published, depicting the hard lives led by shop-assistants.
A novel called *Life behind the Counter* was reviewed at length
in one paper, and ended with a piece of plain speaking:

"The Early Closing Movement rests mainly with ladies

to retard or accelerate. If there were not late customers, harsh and avaricious shopkeepers would have no temptation to keep late hours, and ruin the health, mental and bodily, of their unfortunate dependents."

The advertisements in the newspapers of the first half of the nineteenth century give an idea of the amplitude of life then: of silks bought by the dozen yards, flour by the sack, sauces by the pottle (a two-gallon measure). There was a rich choice of foods and spices, of sauces and appetizers—reindeer tongues and elderflower water, samphire and red capsicum, 'piccalilla' and Dr Kitchiner's Zest.

From food to finery, from gloves to three-decker novels, from "A pretty cottage in Islington at £10 per annum" to "Bonnets trimmed unsparingly with ribbons, ruchings, and flowers"—there is an endless variety in the closely printed columns.

One advertisement stands out. It appears constantly, insistently, and it is not concerned with life, but with death. "Bombazines, velvets, crapes, widows' bands, and a profusion of garments with which to mark the melancholy occasion," says the Mourning Warehouse, and goes on to state the degree of mourning required by relatives, ending with those of farthest kinship.

The fetish of deep family mourning was encouraged by the tradesmen concerned; but it was also one of the most strongly entrenched customs of the age. Mourning the dead is an instinct as old as man, but in no era had it become such an iron-bound convention as in the Victorian age. There were nearly as many undertakers' advertisements as those of the mourning warehouses, and the emphasis was all on display. A tradesman's card of the thirties is headed: "At the Naked Boy and Coffin", and is illustrated by an engraving of a cherub standing beside an elaborately decorated coffin. The text gives a list of "horses, carriages, plumes, mutes," and other trappings of woe which could be provided "at a reasonable cost."

The reasonable cost often ran into great sums, and families who could hardly afford to live in any sort of comfort were compelled by the force of their neighbours' opinion to run into debt in order to pay sufficient homage to their dead by providing a grand funeral. The fashionable rich spent huge sums on obsequies, which were reported in detail and copied as far as possible, on a lesser scale, by all classes right down to the artisan.

Attempts were made from time to time to persuade people of the folly of spending so much money on useless show; and at last came an example of reform from an aristocratic quarter. In April 1854 *The Times* said:

"It may not, perhaps, have escaped the public recollection that some eighteen months or two years back, we called attention to the subject of funeral expenses. What can be more monstrous than the taste which dictates these displays? What more outrageous than the system of inflicting heavy burdens and difficulties upon the living, who are yet within reach of the world's troubles, for the sake of those who have just escaped from them? ... To be alone with one's grief is the best until decent composure and self-restraint have resumed their habitual sway. The black horses, the mutes with their faces of three-and-sixpenny commiseration, and all the usual paraphernalia of professional sorrow simply serve to vulgarise feelings which every man would gladly confine within his own breast. The whole arrangement is one of fashion. ... In the middle classes a splendid funeral must be arranged, really for no better reason than because persons more highly placed in the social scale while living, have caused that fashion to be followed, when dead, with respect to their interment.

"To-day we have to record, with no ordinary respect, the directions left by the late Duke of Portland in his will. These were to the effect that he should be buried with as little ceremony as possible, in a country churchyard, and that the expense of his funeral should be limited to £100. The Duke of Portland was a man of enormous wealth, and yet, with singular good taste and propriety, he has made his own case a means of asserting the truth that when the jaws of the grave have closed on a human being there is an end of rank and distinction. ... Those who wish to range themselves on the side of discretion and good taste may henceforth strengthen themselves by his example, and refuse to follow in the beaten track of the mourning coach and six, with all its heavy vulgarity and display. The fashion they set would be followed, because it was the fashion. In hundreds, ay, in thousands of cases every year, poor families would be spared sacrifices which must end in their embarrassment, if not their ruin."

The example may have been followed by a few independently-minded people, but mourning customs had long roots. Fifty years later there were just as many advertisements of the same kind.

FOOD AND HOUSEKEEPING

THERE is an impression that Victorian food was invented
by Mrs Beeton, and that she began every recipe with
"Take a dozen eggs." Isabella Beeton did not, in fact,
become famous until some time after her collection of
recipes was published in book-form—in 1861—after appear-
ing in parts in *The Englishwoman's Domestic Magazine*, which
her husband published.

Mrs Beeton's recipes were economical, not extravagant,
and in this she was following the example of her prede-
cessors. Their recipes gave large quantities of ingredients
because households were large, much entertaining was done
at home, and the two main meals of the day were substantial. Reading through early nineteenth-century cookery
books, one gets the impression not so much of richness and
extravagance as of solid English food, served with appropriate sauces, vegetables, and trimmings. The apparently
lavish recipes were suitable to their period; it was considered
wicked to waste food, and the early Victorian housewife
prided herself on there being no waste in her kitchen.

There were several well-established cookery-books which
went through many editions, two of the best known being
Mrs Rundell's *New System of Domestic Cookery* and Miss
Acton's *Modern Cookery in All Its Branches*. It is said that
Miss Acton was ambitious to write poetry, but a publisher

persuaded her that a good cookery-book would be more useful. If she was as good a poet as she was a recipe-maker Victorian literature is the poorer.

Dr Kitchiner's *Cook's Oracle* is also much quoted in contemporary papers, but Francatelli equalled him in popularity. Francatelli's *A Plain Cookery Book for the Working Classes* showed a sensible and sympathetic understanding of the cheap food which was all a labouring-man could afford. The first recipe which I read when I opened the little paper-backed book began with the heartening words "Warm a pint of beer."

The most famous cook of the day was Alexis Soyer, the chef of the Reform Club, who was later to be such a help and comfort to Florence Nightingale when he went out to the Crimea to reorganize the meals in the hospitals there. He was a man with a strong personality, and an artist as well as a practical craftsman in his profession. His two books *The Gastronomic Regenerator* and *The Modern Housewife*, or *Ménagère*, are perfect examples of the imaginative treatment of food. He gives footnotes explaining the various processes of cooking, and adds information about the origins and uses of spices and condiments with a touch of Gallic humour, addressing the reader as a friend and pupil.

Soyer was known for his readiness to try new methods; his gas-kitchen at the Reform Club was a show-place, and he was always experimenting. In the *Ménagère* he tells of the circumstance which caused him to study an improved way of making coffee:

"Whilst travelling by night in a railway train, and arriving in due time at the station . . . after a tedious journey . . . and after waiting in the refreshment room to be served with some of the boiling liquid which they call coffee, I found it as bad as any human being could possibly make it. . . . I told one of my travelling companions that as soon as I arrived at the Reform Club I would make several experiments to simplify the present method of making coffee, and should I be successful in my researches I should forward him the receipt."

"THE PEDLAR CAME ROUND WITH HIS PACK OF
KNICK-KNACKS . . ." (*Chapter* I)
From a water-colour drawing by Lucien Beschie
[*P.* 27]
By courtesy of the Trustees of the British Museum

Water

Coffe

a Lady who
had been in the
East Indies
showed me this

to be had at Boyde
in Bond Street

J.S.

A NEW IDEA FROM ABROAD

Section
of cover

Steam Coocking
apparatus for
Potatoes

The Steam
is sometimes
made to
descend in
a tube

Boiling water

invented by J. Barlow
of 114 King William Street
1843 City

2 Ft. 6 Inches high

This to warm a Room
20 Feet square, for six pence
in 24 hours.
I sketched these soon after their being invented in 1840.

1 Foot high

for a Carriage
and would only
cost one penny a
day

J.S.

NEW INVENTIONS

From pencil drawings by G. Scharf

65

Soyer made his experiments, and sent the following recipe to his train acquaintance:

"To make Coffee: put two ounces of ground coffee into the stewpan, which set upon the fire, stirring the powder round with the spoon until quite hot, then pour over a pint of boiling water; cover over closely for five minutes, pass it through a cloth, warm again, and serve."

The acquaintance wrote thanking Soyer, and said he never recollected having tasted better coffee. I may add that I am able to confirm his opinion, having followed the same directions!

Foreigners who visited England had often a good deal to say in their diaries and letters about English food and cooking. Theodor Fontane, a young German, spent several years in England between 1844 and 1859, and there are frequent references to food in his letters. Writing to his father in 1852 he describes a meal in an English home, to which he had been invited:

"Luncheon consisted of clear soup, roast beef with Yorkshire pudding, accompanied by sherry, venison pasties, ham with asparagus, plum-pudding, *crême au vin*, orange salad, and port."

On another occasion he was invited to a suburban home where he was kindly entertained, but where the food was of a different order:

"We sat down to dinner. The meal consisted almost entirely of fish and meat. There was also a rice-pudding which could have found no favour in our country any more than would the gooseberry-fool, which was anything but appetizing. . . . The sherry was followed by red-currant and ginger wine, thus making me familiar with beverages which are rarities in Germany, and which I, for one, became acquainted with in England."

Hospitality to strangers, and the entertainment of friends and relations, were recognized and important parts of social life. Theodor Fontane's two meals were typical of the two levels of ordinary middle-class meals: the overflowing menu for an occasion, and the simple, solid dinner of family life.

E

Journals gave recipes "for the household" and "for guests." In one magazine the suggested fare for a party includes:

"A noble round of boiled beef, a turkey, a boiled ham, a pheasant pie, sausage rolls, scalloped oysters, and Stilton cheese; flanked by pale ale, sherry and negus, with fruit, cheesecake and greengage tart."

Negus appears constantly—spiced wine mixed with hot water, which was sometimes served with lumps of sugar.

Cookery-books and recipes in magazines were for the town housewife; in the country, fare was traditional, and usually of the simplest kind. A farmer's wife had the labourers to feed as well as her own menfolk, and there was no time for fancy cooking in her busy day. But during the short periods of slackness between seasons a yeoman farmer liked to have a gathering of relations and friends, and his wife and the dairymaids would spend a week preparing for a feast that was also traditional, and could only be possible in the country.

There would be turkeys, ducks, and chickens—all home-killed, and stuffed with home-made sausage-meat and herbs from the garden. There would be fruit from the orchards: apples and pears and plums and apricots, served fresh if in season, or preserved from the year before. With them would come great bowls of clouted cream; and, to follow, frumenty made from the finest wheaten flour, spiced and thick with raisins; sillabubs and figgy-pudding; saffron-cake, if it was the West country, or open pies, if it was the North. Drinks there would be in plenty: ale and cider, together with home-brews from elderberry and dandelion, parsnip and cowslip and tart cherry, made a year before and left to mature in the cool darkness of the cellar.

Food in early Victorian days was, to our eyes, very cheap; but in order to get a true picture of the cost we must compare food prices with contemporary wages, and not with the very different prices of our own day.

There was no such thing as a basic wage for industry, but one can take about £300 a year as a reasonable figure for a middle-class income, and twenty-five shillings a week for the average artisan. This last appears to be the wage most usually offered in advertisements for superior workmen, clerks, and shopmen. Sometimes it is as low as a guinea, occasionally as high as thirty shillings. But "five-and-twenty shillings and prospects for a sober, respectable individual" is a representative figure. The 'labouring and industrial classes' lived on from ten shillings to a pound a week.

The two most important foods for those existing on low incomes were bread and potatoes. The price of bread was the subject of much bitterness throughout the thirties and early forties, and there was a great deal of hunger in poor homes until the repeal of the Corn Laws, which brought down the price of bread. These laws were passed after the Napoleonic wars, and were designed to protect the farmer at home by forbidding the importation of foreign corn until home-grown corn had reached a certain figure.

The result was dear bread, which was as much as eight-pence-halfpenny a quartern loaf in the early forties; the prices fluctuated with the state of the harvests. An Anti-Corn Law League was founded, mainly by the industrialists in the North, who employed the workpeople most affected by the high prices.

Then came the terrible year of famine in Ireland, 1845, when the potato crop failed—and potatoes were the staple food of the Irish peasant. Frances Power Cobbe, in her *Life*, tells of the tragedy of the day when she drove out from her home to some festivity, passing fields of green, healthy potatoes on the way, and returning by the same fields some hours later and finding them black with rotting plants.

The famine year, and the continued distress of the thousands of families who could not afford to buy enough bread for their needs, helped the Anti-Corn Law Leaguers in their campaign, and the Corn Laws were repealed in 1846. Prices did not immediately fall, but by 1848 a quartern loaf was down to sixpence, and in the following year it was fivepence halfpenny.

People were heavy meat-eaters; the largest item in the weekly budget was butcher's meat. Three pounds of meat per

week for each person is not an unusual amount noted in old
housekeeping books. Beef or mutton was sixpence a pound,
and eightpence for the best cuts; an ox-tongue cost three
and sixpence, rabbits one and sixpence, and hares half a
crown. A turkey or a goose cost about eight shillings, and
a chicken less; while a young sucking-pig could be bought
at a farm for a sovereign.

With butter at ninepence a pound, the early Victorian
woman could make the rich biscuits and cakes which were
served with wine to afternoon callers; five-o'clock tea did
not come in until much later in the century. Tea was drunk
at any time of the day, and was extremely popular with all
classes of society. Its quality varied with the price; "common tea" was about three shillings a pound, and went up to
the finest Orange Pekoe at eight shillings. Coffee from
Ceylon was one and fourpence a pound, and real Mocha two
shillings.

There were few special foods for infants and children
on sale at the grocer's; the Victorian mother believed in
plainness and plenty as the best fare for her young family.
They had bread and butter, preserves, vegetable soup, rice-
pudding, potatoes, and "well-boiled cabbage." When they
were ill they were given water-gruel and pap—bread
soaked in milk.

This early training in what a digestion could get used to
must have stood them in good stead when they came later
to face the meals for grown-ups in the dining-room. But
that would have been no consolation to the youth in Mrs
Turner's *Cautionary Stories* who asked:

> "Mama, why mayn't I, when I dine,
>   Eat ham and goose, and drink port-wine?
> And why mayn't I, as well as you,
>   Eat pudding, soup, and mutton too?"

> *Answer*
> "Because, my dear, it is not right
>   To spoil the youthful appetite."

The solid fare in nursery and schoolroom was lightened
in a great many homes by a plentiful supply of fruit. Most

houses in the country or on the fringes of the towns had orchards or gardens with apple-, pear-, and plum-trees, and as it was beginning to be recognized that "a sufficiency of fruit cleanses the blood of the young" children were allowed that sufficiency. Fruit was cheap to buy; it was grown in market-gardens outside most towns, and brought in on donkey-carts in the early mornings. Fruits from abroad were also imported in quantity. One old house-keeping book has an item, "Five oranges, one penny," and another, "A large bag of apricots, 4*d*."

Eating out of doors was a favourite summer habit of the Victorian family; a picnic was a popular jaunt. Meat-pies and sandwiches formed the solid part of the meal, and "cos lettuce, well washed, parted, and wrapped in a clean linen cloth" was also a contribution to an alfresco meal. If the family went far afield in their own gig or pony-cart the food would be packed in a hamper, together with the rugs and wraps and guide-books.

The small, easily carried luncheon basket was an invention of Scott's, the London basket-makers, for use at the Great Exhibition. They realized that thousands of people who came up to London to see the Exhibition would find difficulty in getting meals at the crowded restaurants, and they devised a portable basket, fitted with compartments, which a person could pack at home and carry with ease. The idea caught on, and was immensely successful.

The chop-houses and oyster-shops which abounded in London and the big cities were patronized mostly by men, but ladies might have meals out at respectable eating-houses, where they could choose a substantial dinner of beefsteak-pie, or soles brought in from the coast that day. The actual food—the meat, the fish,—would be of good quality. The cooking would be a matter of controversy.

English cooking was even then becoming a butt for *Punch* and foreign satirists. It was attacked as being heavy, prepared without imagination, and responsible for the less admirable aspects of the English character. An editorial in the *Lancet* in 1851 went farther:

"The province of a medical journalist being chiefly to

discuss questions connected with the health and physical condition of individuals ... our present remarks are confined to the influence [which] improperly prepared food exerts in the production of disease; and also to enquire how far the inhabitants of England would gain by adopting a few of the culinary maxims contained in the peptic vocabularies of other countries, particularly of France, where cookery has been cultivated, if not actually classed, as a science. . . . In south Britain, notwithstanding the productions of nature, both animal and vegetable, consumed as food, are often superior to the same kinds of materials used in most Continental nations, the mode of preparing them for the human stomach is frequently exceedingly defective."

The *Lancet* also attacked the commercial practice of adulterating foods, then very prevalent. There were no Food Acts, and a dishonest grocer could increase his stock of ground cereals, teas, coffees, and other commodities by adulteration, knowing he was unlikely to be prosecuted even if he were exposed. The *Lancet* published a long series of articles, illustrated by diagrams and tables, showing in detail how adulteration was carried out, and giving facts about the dangerous effects of alum and other substances used. The housewife was unlikely to read the *Lancet*, but newspapers quoted from these articles at great length, and so she was given some warning.

Housekeeping was a serious subject in early Victorian days. It was the theme of many books of advice, often written by "A Lady," and addressed to the inexperienced wife presumably anxious to have her mistakes corrected. Many of these books were written in dialogue form, apparently between a congenital idiot (the young wife) and a perfect housekeeper (the author). "A Lady" usually began on a high moral plane, advised a firm manner towards servants, a good table for one's husband, and unremitting private devotions.

Other guides were equally uplifting, but more practical. Mrs Parkes's *Domestic Duties*, the fourth edition of which was published in 1837, is a solidly bound volume in calf, and covers every department of housekeeping, and a good deal else besides. Together with instructions on marketing, the keeping of stores, furnishing, cooking, carving, cleaning, and dealing with "insects of no pleasing description," Mrs Parkes has vigorous opinions on "Conduct to be observed towards former friends," the choice of new acquaintances for a newly married woman, the desirability of showing all correspondence to a husband, principles of conduct, pride and vanity, and how to deal with one's mother-in-law.

A popular type of book was James Luckcock's *Hints for Practical Economy in the Management of Household Affairs*, in which there are tables of expenses for incomes from a guinea a week to £400 a year.

In the lowest table "eatables" for a man, wife, and two children are given as fourpence a day, and rent as two shillings a week. On an income of £100 a year the table is:

		s. d.	
Rent		4.6	*per week*
Eatables (6*d.* a day each) .		14.0	
Beer and Liquors . .		3.3	
Clothing, Man . .		4.6	
Ditto, Woman . .		2.3	
Ditto, two children .		1.2	
Coals		2.0	
Washing . . .		2.0	
Levies and Taxes . .		1.4	
Subscriptions . .		7	
Schooling . . .		9	
Occasional Servant .		9	
Wear and Tear . .		1.4	

An income of £300 brings a cautious extension of items:

	£	s. d.	
Rent		11.6	*per week*
Eatables (with visitors) .	1	1.2	
Beer, wines, spirits, etc .		9.7	
Clothing, Man . .		7.0	
Clothing, Woman .		4.6	

	£ s. d.	
Clothing, Two children .	4.6	*per week*
Coals	3.6	
Washing . . .	3.10	
Levies and Taxes . .	4.6	
Subscriptions . .	3.3	
Schooling . . .	15.4	
Servants (wages £7, board £15)	8.5	
Household linen, etc. .	3.3	
Garden . . .	3.3	
Amusements . .	2.3	
Stationery and newspapers	1.6	
Insurance, repairs, etc.	2.3	
Doctor . . .	1.2	
Wear and Tear . .	3.10	

Luckcock stressed the importance of the housekeeper living within her income; he himself had been one of a family of five children whom his parents had brought up on a total income of £80 a year, and he declared that by careful management and never falling into debt they had managed very well.

A popular 'inquire within' type of book published about 1850 was *The Household Book of Domestic Economy*, which contained fifteen hundred "practical receipts in Cookery, the Arts, Manufactures, and Trades, including Medicine, Pharmacy, etc." One could, on a single page, learn how to make a Suet Crust for Pies, Gunpowder, Artificial Asses' Milk, and Economical Bread. Another page gave recipes for Stewed Tomatoes, dealt with Depression of the Spirits, suggested a Treatment for Epilepsy and a method of Clearing Rose Trees from Blight, and gave directions on how to Roast a Hare. This was followed by a dissertation on the Incrustation of Boilers. A little farther on came a short essay on Shaving: "This is a very simple operation (the difficulty all lies in the razor), and easy to perform. The face must be clean, for a razor is not made to scrape road-sand away."

Another book of advice addressed to young housewives

was written from a different point of view; it did not contain recipes, but was "a practical enquiry into what chiefly mars or makes the comfort of domestic life," and was called: *Home Truths for Home Peace, or, Muddle Defeated*. The author attacked the snobbery which made young wives of modest means ape their richer sisters by having houses too large for them and too much furniture, so that the house-work was never done. A small house suited to one's means, with everything in order, was the ideal demanded by this Lady. Especially did she advise the setting aside of a Gentle-man's Room, no matter how small the house:

"Important above almost every other arrangement in your establishment is the consecration of one room to the especial use of the master of the house. A sound and lovely policy is that which secures to a husband certain privileges and comforts that he can never find elsewhere, and are calcu-lated to counterbalance the weight of the many other attractions which his immediate circle cannot offer. . . . It will keep him from clubs and card-parties, and prove a sanctuary from the numerous petty domestic troubles and annoyances that, as few men can comprehend or tolerate, it is much better they should not see."

The author went on to advise the young mistress of the household to have "the observing eye, the calculating head, the skilful hand, the concise speech, the gentle step, the external tidiness, and the internal purification," which were necessary qualifications for good housekeeping. After a recommendation to use Liquid Glue for fractured furniture "A Lady" returned to her main theme:

"The constant exercise of patience and forbearance is never more necessary or praiseworthy than in domestic life. . . . Narrow means, an inconvenient house, tiresome chil-dren, or, worse even than these, toothache and an ill-tem-pered husband—these are trials for which patience is the best and almost only remedy."

VII

FASHION

THE Early Victorian period in dress may fairly be called
the age of the petticoat, for that garment determined
the line of the mode for years, until its multiplication
led in the end to the invention of the crinoline frame. The
crinoline did not come in with the accession of the young
queen. In 1837 the wide skirts, like great bells, were supported by six or seven petticoats, the under ones of scalloped
flannel, the top two of stiffly starched muslin or cotton.

In the latter days of the Regency, skirts had been several
inches off the ground, showing neat, square-toed slippers
with flat soles. By the forties they hid the ankles, and by
1850 fashion had lowered them to the ground. Doctors
wrote to the papers, asking if it were healthy for women to
turn themselves into human brooms; and Joseph Paxton's
good-natured satirical shaft at the fashion was widely
quoted in 1851. Replying to a speech of welcome at a ban-
quet held at Richmond, in Surrey, on the occasion of the
Great Exhibition, Paxton said he had fancied the Crystal
Palace would be a difficult place to keep clean. He had
designed a machine of a hundred-housemaid power to
obviate that inconvenience, and he had put the Commissioners to some expense in having these machines made.
They had not, however, been called into requisition, for the
building had been kept completely clean by the rich silk
dresses of the ladies.

The line of the dress remained substantially the same during most of the early Victorian period. The bodice was moulded smoothly to the figure, lined and heavily boned to keep its shape. It came up to the throat for day wear, and was cut in a straight *décolletage* for the evening. Sleeves were narrow, in contrast to the enormous balloon sleeves of the early thirties; these had been modified by degrees until they were plain and straight, widening a little at the wrists to show an undersleeve of fine lace or cambric. In the late forties and early fifties there was a vogue for alternative bodices to a gown, a long-sleeved, high-necked bodice for day, and a low-cut one for evening. As the bodice with its boned, pointed front fitted snugly over the skirt, the change-over was simple.

The close-fitting bodice, the point, the increasing fullness of the skirt—all were designed to enhance the apparent smallness of the waist. I suggest "apparent" because there is evidence that the legendary seventeen-inch Victorian waist was more often than not a successful optical illusion, helped by clever designing. Doris Langley Moore, in her book *The Woman in Fashion*, says that of the many hundreds of Victorian dresses which have passed through her hands she has never come across a single specimen with a seventeen-inch waist. Most of the Victorian costumes in her collection fit women of normal size to-day, and she adds that it has been necessary to 'take in' more frequently than to 'let out.'

There was a great deal of tight-lacing—not a surprising fact considering the amount of underclothing women wore; without some control they would have had thirty-inch waist-lines to their dresses. Besides the half-dozen petti-coats a woman wore a shift, or full chemise, fine-linen drawers, and a petticoat-bodice. The corset itself was a sturdy affair which reached from the top of the bust to half-way down the hips.

The subject of tight-lacing raged through the newspapers and journals of the forties and fifties. One writer declared:

"There would be no tight-lacing if girls could be made to understand this simple fact, that men dread the thought of marrying a woman who has fits of irritable temper, bad headaches and other ailments, all of which are the first products of the compression of the waist."

The most earnest warnings came from doctors, who tried to frighten women into stopping the practice. In the *Ladies' Pocket Magazine*, 1837, there is a review of a book by a doctor which got prominent notices in several papers. This was William Coulson's *Deformities of the Chest and Spine*, and the reviewer says:

"We would earnestly recommend the perusal of a work under the above title to that portion of our readers which have a rising family of daughters. It presents a faithful but melancholy portrait of the organic evils which result from the injurious practice of tight stay-lacing. Among the frightful complaints which this system is the source, are enumerated cancer and consumption. Mr Coulson simply and distinctly describes the method by which the baneful consequences of physical mal-formation may be remedied. His book is illustrated with plates of the human structure, which at once show the superior symmetry of the form which has not been compressed by stays, to that of the deluded votary of a vain and destructive habit. . . . To use means for contracting the space necessary for containing the machinery of the human frame is very like presumption; and we hope yet to see the period when fashion will expel the folly of tight-lacing."

The stay-makers were not slow to use the health motif in pushing their wares. An advertisement in 1850 combines a sense of responsibility with pride in an original idea:

"Some months ago we attempted to draw attention to the subject of corsets, and endeavoured to show that health, no less than good taste, was a point to be considered in reference to them. But within these six months, still further improvements have been made, and we feel it a duty to mention two sorts of Corsets which are already registered, and have been prepared for the Great Exhibition.

"*The Corset Amazone* is quite a triumph of invention. By aid of elastic lacings, it yields to every respiration or movement of the equestrian, and may be worn long or short at pleasure. The touch of a silken cord curtails by about three inches the length of the corset, and thus reduces the ordinary stay to a riding one in a moment.

"*The Corset à la Nourrice* is intended for ladies who are fulfilling the dearest offices of maternity, and by a simple arrangement obviates every usual annoyance and inconvenience. It is not very easy to describe this corset, but we may observe that by the withdrawal of two slender bones, an entire gusset is removed—but may be replaced with equal expedition. For obvious reasons it is an advantage to be provided with an extra pair of gussets."

By the end of the forties skirts had become so full and heavy that a woman of leisure appeared to glide along, self-impelled by her far-spreading dress. Its amplitude was not always supported entirely by petticoats; there were "deceivers" of plaited horsehair, sewn to the top of the underskirt to make the dress stand away from the figure and so diminish the waist. A trade-card of the period advertises an unexpected aid to fullness. The engraved illustration shows a petticoat which has a kind of bicycle inner-tube attached round its hem, with the description, "The New Jupon Ballon Petticoat with Inflating Tubes."

The crinoline appeared in the early eighteen-fifties. It was a light, pliant framework of graduated steel hoops, and it became popular immediately, doing away with the necessity of wearing masses of petticoats, yet retaining the fashionable line. It must have given the early Victorian woman a feeling of buoyancy as she moved about in her tilting frame, with her legs free inside—decently booted and stockinged, of course. The swaying crinoline showed a lady's ankles when she walked, and half-boots and substantial stockings were soon produced.

Fashion has never been unduly influenced by convenience and the crinoline came into favour at a time when women were beginning to travel about more than they had ever done before. *Punch* was full of cartoons showing crinolined ladies trying to board omnibuses or being stuck in the doorway of a railway carriage. Cooks in crinolines were shown in their kitchens, accidentally sweeping crockery from table to floor as they turned to see a horrified 'missus' standing at the door. But ridicule did not have any effect on the fashion; the crinoline grew ever wider.

In 1851 an article appeared in *Eliza Cook's Journal* headed "Revolution in Ladies' Dress." It ran:

"The ladies in the United States threaten an entire revolution in the fashion of female dress. . . . Every surgeon knows well enough what destruction to female life and health have been caused by the use of stays and corsets, since the popular notion of being charming has been confined to a hand-breadth of tightly compressed ribs and liver. . . . What would the ladies say to . . . adopting the new American female dress? The upper garment is loose-fitting, and reaches to the knees; underneath are loose trowsers reaching to the ancles. The new dress is greatly approved by those who wear it. If the long draggling dresses, which Mr Paxton alleges have kept the Exhibition swept clean since its opening, are unhealthy and uncomfortable, besides being ungraceful, surely it is time to meditate a reform, and the American lady has done well to take the lead."

The Annual Register for June of that year gives a fair summary of the general reaction to Amelia Bloomer's historic invention. In a report headed "Female Costume—the Bloomers" it said:

"Among the matters which require to be chronicled, not because of their intrinsic importance but on account of the interest they excite at the time, an attempted revolution in female dress which at the time caused much amusement, must not be passed over. It was introduced from America, . . . [and was] very like the dress worn by schoolgirls who are intrusted with a hoop and stick. . . . A few dashing damsels—of what character is unknown—sported the hybrid garments in some public places; but the dress having been adopted by women whose character was not at all doubtful, and by barmaids of public houses, the absurdity died away."

The amusement was given a lead by *Punch*, which had

something here much to its taste. Normally sympathetic to every movement aimed at the abolition of abuses, especially those which affected women, *Punch* thought Amelia Bloomer was carrying this particular reform too far. It had several weeks of light-hearted larking with the idea of women wearing trousers, and asked if they would not like to take over men's occupations too? One cartoon showed women police fainting in a graceful group at the first hint of a street row; another showed a woman barrister in wig and gown. *Punch* laughed, the public laughed with it, and the sensation died away. Women's "trowsers" were forgotten, together with other old jokes.

The most distinctive outdoor garment of the period was the shawl, which had come into fashion at the beginning of the century, and was in vogue for forty years. Increasing trade with India brought cargoes of beautiful cashmere shawls to the English shops. Paisley shawls were equally popular. The quality of many of these shawls can be appreciated to-day, for there are superb specimens in collections in different parts of the country, and many others are heirlooms in private families.

The shawl was usually large enough to be worn as a warm wrap, the point of its folded three-corner shape reaching well over the skirt at the back. The pelisse, a wrap which dated from the early eighteen-hundreds, was a fitted version of the shawl. The mantle, another variation, was shaped and lined, and sometimes had a roomy hood attached which a lady could draw over her bonnet for rain.

A merchant in St Paul's Churchyard brought out a novelty in 1852, a circular shawl, the design being printed on it instead of woven into it:

"It is something between a shawl and a mantle, and the hood, which is usually attached, may be removed at pleasure. These Circular Shawls show the figure and yet shroud it, and are warm as well as light. Being registered, they are not yet made in coarse materials, and therefore are not likely to become common. We may warn our readers that the effect produced by these shawls is very different from that obtained by the home manufacture of a shawl into a mantle—a feat we have once or twice known attempted with most signal failure."

Besides the mantle, there was the mantelet, a shorter variation with long, scarf-like ends. A fashion writer of the early fifties drops a discreet hint that these are "extremely pretty for married ladies, but not quite youthful enough for *demoiselles*."

Cloaks, with or without hoods, were worn at all times of the day, the *bournouse*, a copy of the Arab dress, becoming fashionable in the fifties. By 1857 the shaped cape reaching to below the waist was a favourite line; the cape was often made of silk plush or velvet, and was heavily embroidered in braid, beads, and fringe.

Fur does not appear very much in outdoor fashions for the middle-class woman except as an occasional trimming. The fur cloak or pelisse is mentioned by magazine correspondents who keep an eye on the *haute monde*, but, as one of these ladies remarks, "sable is a costly pelt," and she does not put it forward as a serious pointer to fashion. "The respectable dame," she adds, "must be content with seal-skin or mink."

The bonnet, like the crinoline and shawl-shaped outer garments, was characteristic of a woman's costume throughout the period. Its line varied a little, but its basic shape was the same. In the early forties the brim was large, and framed the face; the size gradually diminished into the small bonnet worn half-way back on the head and finished off with a tiny 'curtain' behind, the fashion of the fifties.

Bonnets were apt to be heavily overtrimmed with cascades of ribbon and masses of flowers and feathers; but at their simplest, set off with a lining of quilled lace and flower-buds, they could be exceedingly becoming. They were expensive to buy and were often made at home. The crown, or capote, was gathered on to a cane or whalebone foundation, which could be bought at the milliner's; the handbooks of millinery and dressmaking give instructions, with diagrams, for making "modish caps and bonnets."

A DOUBTFUL CASE—THE ROAD TO ALDERSHOTT

LADY: Can I pass, Soldier?
IMPUDENT SENTRY: Well, I really can't say, Ma'am, but there was a waggon-load of hay went through about five minutes since.

(No. 5 of Read's Crinoline Sketches)

From the author's collection

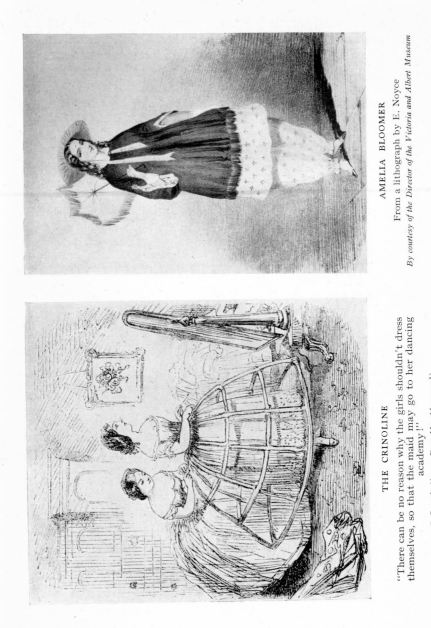

THE CRINOLINE

"There can be no reason why the girls shouldn't dress themselves, so that the maid may go to her dancing academy!"

J. Leech (from *Punch's Almanack*)

AMELIA BLOOMER

From a lithograph by E. Noyce

By courtesy of the Director of the Victoria and Albert Museum

Caps were important, for the Victorian woman usually wore one indoors. It was made of net, muslin, or lace, with lappets at each side, like a spaniel's ears. House-caps were trimmed with ribbons and flowers, and were often exquisitely embroidered.

Both the caps and bonnets perfectly suited the *coiffures* of the time; the bunched corkscrew curls worn framing the cheeks, and the back-hair dressed in a flat chignon. In the fifties the side-curls disappeared, and the hair was brushed smoothly down from a centre parting, with a slight fulness over the ears. Thick braids were worn round the back of the head; or, if the hair was not long enough for plaits, it was arranged in a bun or coaxed into an inverted saucer of curls. The changing size of the bonnet naturally had an effect on the manner of dressing the hair; a fashion writer in 1852 states:

"The new bonnets are to be round and close . . . the *capotte* is extremely small, so much so, that the hair will have to be dressed to suit it, being twisted or plaited tightly in a small circle at the back."

Gloves and mittens were important items in a lady's wardrobe. They were worn in the home as well as out of doors, and were an unmistakable mark of gentility, indicating that their wearer had no need to use her hands, which must be protected and kept white. The light colours of the gloves—white, lavender, pearl-grey—added implicitly to the suggestion.

There was a variety of dress accessories which had this same effect of pointing social levels. In the thirties and forties little shoulder-capes in differing styles were very fashionable: pelerines and delerines, canezous and berthes. They were made of lace or embroidered muslin, intricately sewn, and they were solely decorative—examples of what Veblen, the social historian, called Conspicuous Consumption (of labour).

Long scarves or stoles of lace, hand-made collars and tambour-embroidered undersleeves, *vestes* and *gilets*—all were costly additions to a woman's dress. Artificial flowers trimmed caps and bonnets, walking-dresses and *grandes*

F

toilettes, and were worn in the hair by matrons as well as maidens at balls and soirées. The flower-makers of Paris were famous, and their chief market was London. A correspondent of one magazine wrote from Paris:

"We know two young sisters who, from their childhood, have studied this beautiful art . . . the blossoms they make look as if a human hand could hardly have touched them. The skill of these young girls has obtained for them certain privileges; the head gardener of the Jardin des Plantes has given them permission to select specimens of the rarest plants and flowers in that beautiful collection to copy, which they do with an exactitude that is really inconceivable."

The materials of early Victorian dresses make a rich, rustling pattern in the imagination. Brocades, satins, *gros de Naples*, crystalline gauze, organdie, embroidered tulle, taffetas, *pou de soie*, antique moire, transparent muslins— a ballroom must have looked like an exotic garden as the great skirts swung out in quadrille or polka.

Some materials appear in the fashion-news year after year. *Barège* is one—a thin fabric of woven silk and worsted, or cotton and worsted. It was used for morning and afternoon gowns, and was not expensive; an advertisement in 1840 gives the following comparative prices: "Striped and Checked Silks at 18s. 6d. the full dress. French and English Barèges at 5s. 9d. and 8s. 9d. the full dress. Brocaded *Pouse de Soies* at 37s. 6d. the full dress." Merino and *mousseline-de-laine* also appear from year to year, and there are many poplins and twills, foulards and velvets.

Cashmere—apart from its use in shawls—was always in the mode, and was liked for formal afternoon robes as well as for morning wear. It was thin as well as warm, and, in the opinion of one journal, "it submits admirably to embroidery." A white cashmere cloak, hooded and lined with cerise silk, must indeed have justified the opinion that it was "elegant, tasteful, and in no need of superfluous ornamentation when worn by a blooming *demoiselle*."

Scotch plaids were often described as "interesting,"

"original," and "striking." Original many of them certainly were, and would not have been owned by a self-respecting clan. Any fancy check, however patterned, was called a Scotch plaid, and these designs appeared in *glacé* silks as well as in woven woollen stuffs. Queen Victoria doubtless popularized plaids after she took Balmoral as one of her homes, but they appear quite often in the fashion notes of pre-Balmoral days.

For summer, muslins were first favourite: printed, spotted, quadrilled, sprigged, or embroidered in bouquets. Tarlatan was popular for "unmarried girls and youthful matrons," and chintz-patterned cottons were used for morning dresses and for *peignoirs*.

In the early fifties materials for elegant occasions got richer as skirts grew wider over the new crinoline frame. The silk manufacturers in France produced extravagant stuffs to dazzle the wives of the prosperous English merchants. *Soie nacre* had a sheen which resembled mother-of-pearl; *soie cristal* had the effect of "a rich coloured silk, partly veiled by a thin sheet of ice"; *velours mauresques* was "a very stout silk of a black ground, with brown Moorish patterns, a ladylike and original material." The *reps de Jupiter* was in a different style: "The pattern represents thunderbolts, serpentining in flame-colour upon a black or brown ground."

The colours of materials had not the range of later years; vegetable dyes were used until the fifties, and though many of the tints were soft and beautiful the colour-chart was limited. White, pale shades of blue or pink, and yellow were usual for evening dresses, with violet, lavender, and pearl-grey for matrons, and puce, antelope, and chestnut-brown for "dignified elderly ladies."

A great change came into the colour-range after 1856, for in that year William Perkin, a chemist, discovered a process of making aniline dyes from coal-tar. The colours produced in the first few years were crude, which perhaps accounts for the belief that the mid-Victorian woman had a taste for the garish. The magentas, bright reds, and harsh greens associated with her date from the end of the fifties; in time these early colours were subdued, and subsequent experiment led to a great variety of shades later in the century.

Children's clothes in the early Victorian period must have been more uncomfortable to wear than at any other time in history, save perhaps in the Elizabethan period. The stove-pipe trousers and tight short coats or shapeless tunics of the boys, the miniature mound of petticoats and fitted bodices of the girls, can be seen in many collections. Boys and girls were dressed alike up to the age of five, a custom which drew fire from *Punch* in 1847. Under a cartoon depicting a boy in flounces and a girl in trousers, came this attack:

"The infant population of the day may fairly call for re-dress. . . . No salad, no lobster, no anything within our experience was ever submitted to such an incongruous sort of dressing as the present, in which our boys and girls are fitted out. . . . It is difficult for us to distinguish our daughters from our sons, and, by leading us to confound one sex with the other, may urge us to the extremity of confounding the children altogether.

"We revolt against the tyrant fashion which envelopes our boys in the flounced trappings of what should be female finery, and disguises our girls in the sack-like paletot of boyhood. . . . Why do not the arbiters of fashion take a lesson from Nature, who dresses everything appropriately? Nature has as good reason to deck the asparagus with the foliage of the rhubarb as we have to dress our sons in the draperies suited to our daughters."

Starched and flannel petticoats, long pantalettes and stockings, preserved decorum at one end of a little girl, but her bodice was cut as low as her mother's, even in winter. Some attempt was made to change this fashion. Said the *Ladies' Handbook* in 1843:

"Frocks for little girls are, by some persons, directed to be made to come high up to the neck. This is, in our opinion, a practice that should be avoided. The body [bodice] on the contrary should be rather low, and made to lay firmly on the projecting part of the shoulder. . . . The graceful form of the bust should by no means be concealed;

a neat necklace is its proper adornment. Should it be said
that a high neck is necessary on the score of health, nothing
could be farther from the truth. In fact, a moderate expo-
sure to the action of the sun and air is essential to the possession of good health. The notion that to cover up the neck
and bosom of a little girl will prevent her taking cold is
ridiculous in the extreme. It is the most likely way we know
to secure the evil it is intended to avoid. We hope that all
mothers who may read our observations will at once
abandon the idea of high-bodied frocks being in any way con-
ducive to the health and comfort of their female children."

In that same year a girl who was being hardened off above
the waist would probably be wearing enough material to
keep six children of a future generation warm: a linen
chemise, a stay-bodice, drawers to the ankles or short
drawers together with pantalettes which tied above the
knee, two flannel petticoats and two of starched muslin, all
topped by a three-tiered dress stiff with frills and flounces.

Children's clothes were often made at home; the fashion-
books gave diagrams and instructions. It was before the day
of the paper-pattern, which did not come in until the early
sixties, being thought out then by the enterprising Samuel and
Isabella Beeton for their *Englishwoman's Domestic Magazine*.

The sewing-machine was not available for the ordinary
housewife, either. It had been originally invented in the
eighteenth century, but the first real working model was not
made until 1830, when it was patented by the Frenchman
Thimonier. Elias Howe, in America, patented a lockstitch
machine in 1846, and this was developed and began to be
used by the clothing trade. A sewing-machine was shown
at the Great Exhibition, but it did not come into general
home use until well into the sixties.

The early Victorian housewife and the weekly sempstress, unaware of mechanical aids to sewing, made all those
petticoats and pantalettes by hand—hems, seams, gussets,
tucks, gathers, frills, and feather-stitched bands. Little of
their sewing was meant to be seen, but it was done with a
strength and beauty which lasted, to become an inspiration
to later generations of women.

VIII

LEISURE

Sewing—Letter-writing—Music: the Home Performer—Dancing—Sketching—Magazines for Women—Sport: Riding, Skating, Archery

Every Lady should know how to Knit, Net, Knot, and Tat.

From a contemporary women's magazine

IT is difficult to think of the early Victorian woman as ever being idle. She had many hours of leisure after attending to her household, and she filled them with a variety of pursuits. What those were depended on the kind of person she was; the woman with an independent mind and a taste for affairs must have found knitting, netting, knotting, and tatting intolerable. But the ordinary middle-class housewife was content to occupy herself with needlework, to develop any talents or social gifts she might have, and to exchange calls, visits, and parties with friends in her own station of life.

Sewing was a necessary accomplishment for a woman. There was a great pride in plain sewing: hemming with tiny stitches, gathering and 'stroking' cambric into even folds. Morning gowns, as well as underclothing, were usually made at home, with the aid of a sewing-woman who came for four or five shillings a day and her meals. The mistress of the house would sit with her for an hour or two, helping with the plain sewing and no doubt learning a few tricks of the trade.

Hand-made lace was often made at home too. Many beautiful specimens exist in museums and in private families; a handkerchief border shown to me, together with the "receipt," had a foundation-pattern of Italian braid joined together with "Venetian bars" and was "edged with Sorrento stitch", all worked with a fine sewing-needle. The Bethnal Green Museum, in London, has in its collection a number of delicately worked baby-clothes trimmed with hand-made lace of the early Victorian period.

Patchwork was very popular in the thirties and forties, and a quilt was often a family affair, as this passage from a letter written in 1850 indicates: "Mama, Louise, Barbie, and I finished the setting together of my patch bed-cover. I am pleased." The pieces, lozenge-shaped or six-sided, were cut out of old dresses or were often bought for a shilling a bag from dressmakers' workrooms. The shapes were tacked over paper and 'set' in patterns, some of them very intricate; they were then sewn together on the wrong side, and the paper removed.

There was not so much cross-stitch done as in the first two decades of the century, though girls were still taught the stitch on samplers. An old lady, recalling in her journal the days of her girlhood, says of her life in 1843, when she was ten years old: "I was taught to sew the alphabet in cross-stitches on a piece of fine canvas, so that I could mark my wedding linen when the time came."

Plain knitting was not in vogue, except duty knitting for the poor; but berlin-work, a form of fancy knitting, was fashionable. The magazines of the day gave instructions for making mats, chair-seats, and sofa-backs in berlin-work, with minutely worked-out diagrams and coloured plates.

Fringe-making was also described as a ladylike occupation, together with bead-work on velvet, "especially suitable for a gentleman's smoking-cap of a refined yet masculine design." There was a good deal of crochet, both in card-cases, antimacassars, and doilies, but it was not such a favourite as either netting or tatting. Both these crafts were done with small shuttles. Purses were netted in silk and lined with a contrasting colour. Tatting produced a fine crochet effect, and was used for cuffs and collars and the 'falls' which trimmed the sides of a fancy cap.

Needlework by no means occupied all a woman's leisure time. She spent several hours every week in regular letter-writing. To be a good correspondent was considered a well-bred woman's duty. Letters between members of a family living at a distance from each other was a well-established habit, but an expensive one: a letter cost from twopence to one and eightpence, according to the weight and the distance carried, and was paid for by the recipient. The introduction of the Penny Post in 1840, with a pre-paid stamp, sent up the volume of postal business, and family letters become even more of an institution, full of news, views, gossip, and observations on current events. These letters, embracing as they do a family's kinsmen and connexions, neighbours and friends, bring out for us very vividly the domestic detail of everyday life in that age.

It was a necessary accomplishment for a woman to have good handwriting, especially when thin notepaper was used and lines of writing were crossed at right-angles in order to get as much as possible on to one sheet—a habit from the days of costly postage. Good manners demanded legible penmanship, which accounts for the beauty and character of much Victorian handwriting.

Clear speaking was also considered desirable in a gentlewoman, and there are many references in contemporary journals to the teaching of good diction to the young. There were academies for the "correct use of the voice in the pulpit, on the stage, at the Bar, and in private conversation." There was also uninhibited criticism:

"The English gentlewoman who speaks articulately, pronounces elegantly, and reads with emphasis and discretion is rare. May we earnestly recommend to the mothers, wives, daughters, sisters, aunts, and cousins of England to ponder upon this. It is rude to speak so that no one can hear you. It is vulgar to mumble. It is affected to drawl. It is silly to imitate some fashionable actor or actress. It is a disgrace to leave the meaning of the matter read to the ingenuity of the listener. There is no language so cruelly maltreated as her Majesty's English by her Majesty's well-educated subjects."[1]

More important than the development of the speaking voice were lessons in singing, the showiest of all a young

[1] *Mrs Grundy's Commonplace Book.*

woman's accomplishments. She was taught to play upon
the pianoforte, the harp, and the guitar; but few girls took
these instruments seriously, except for the purpose of
accompanying songs. The 'music' which played so large a
part in the Victorian girl's leisure was singing—the learning
of ballads, hundreds of which were published every year.

My Home is in the Valley below, *In Dreams Thou'rt with
me still*, *Dost Thou forget?*—these were typical. A girl with
good articulation might try something on a higher flight:

> E'en as of old Amphion's tuneful string
> Made walls and turrets to his verse unspring,
> So in our hearts the poet's simple lays
> Bulwarks of Beauty and of Truth may raise;
> Whose walls, impregnable and pure, may dare
> The shafts of sin—the darts of wild despair.
>
> And e'en as Orpheus, with his silvery song,
> Drew to his music stubborn brutes along,
> So in our hearts the poet's power may draw
> In mute obedience to harmonious law
> Our passions wild—and with celestial lays
> Our grovelling senses to Elysium raise.

To this a gentleman of the party might well reply:

> Hail! Flower so stately, fair, and bright,
> That sheddest from thy petals white,
> On our parterre such beams of light,
>   White Lily!
>
> Emblem of purity and truth,
> Thy snowy charms are fit, in sooth,
> To deck the brow of Christian youth,
>   Fair Lily!
>
> Thy upright bearing, stately crest,
> And golden eye to Heaven addressed
> A native dignity attest,
>   Proud Lily!

The song was ostensibly written to a lily, but when sung
to a young lady the sentiments were unmistakable. The

home performer did not require subtlety or overtones. The requirements for a ballad to be sung in the family circle were expressed in this review of a new song:

"It is a long time since we met with so truly a charming ballad as this. The poetry, expressive of a pretty sentiment, is graceful and flowing, while the melody is of that taking character, which, once heard, is never to be forgotten. . . . The accompaniment, without being difficult, is highly effective. . . . It is published in the key of E, and ranges within the compass of an ordinary voice."

Dancing was as popular as singing, and a party nearly always ended with sets of quadrilles, the galop, schottische, and the polka. If it was a family gathering some one would dash off the music on the piano, but a more formal affair would be attended by a "highly select band of Cornet, Harp, Violin, and Guitar."

One could, of course, take the exercise more seriously, and go to Mr Tenniel, of Gloucester Place, London, who announced to the "nobility, gentry, and his friends, that his course of instruction included Dancing, Deportment, and modified Calisthenics, with his Systolic and Dyastolic Staff." That might not be such light-hearted fun as quadrilles in the parlour at home, but it made an impressive subject of conversation.

Sketching and drawing were leisure-time occupations which were taken for granted, but a woman's chief interest was in reading. It was the heyday of the circulating library, where the works of the great literary figures of the day could be borrowed if she had not already bought them in monthly parts before they were published in the usual three volumes.

Apart from these there was an enormous amount written especially for women: society novels, tales of mystery, highly coloured romances, and improving books like *The Young Lady's Guide through Life to Immortality*, *The Young Wife's Companion*, *A Wife's Duty to her Husband*, and many more of the kind.

There were also the Annuals: *The Keepsake*, *The Book of*

Beauty, The Album Wreath, and others. Beginning in the eighteen-twenties with *The Forget-me-not,* these handsomely bound publications were to be found in every drawing-room. They were edited by fashionable women like the Countess of Blessington and Mrs Norton, and sold by the thousand. Greville called them "gorgeous inanities," and Lockhart referred to them as being of "this toyshop of literature"; but Elizabeth Barrett, Caroline Southey, Thackeray, Dickens, and other notable contributors were found in their pages among many who were mediocre. The Annuals were declining in popularity by the thirties, but they continued to be published for another ten or twenty years.

For more general women's reading the monthly magazines had big sales. There were a good many of them, well printed and produced, and illustrated with engravings and coloured plates. The best-known were *The Lady's Cabinet, The Ladies' Companion,* and *La Belle Assemblée. The Englishwoman's Domestic Magazine,* edited by Samuel Beeton, began to come out in 1852, and soon had a huge circulation. Beeton's wife, Isabella, edited the cookery notes, which were afterwards expanded into her famous work.

These magazines published stories, poems, reviews of current books, critical notes on concerts and plays, and a great many articles on non-domestic subjects: travel, music and painting, the expanding world of science. These were written in no predigested form, but were set out at length and seriously discussed.

The one subject which was skated round and seldom presented in an unbiased spirit was religion. It was extremely difficult for most early Victorians to reconcile the new discoveries in science with religious teaching as they knew it, and writers had to tread delicately. Maria Norris, writing on geology in *La Belle Assemblée* in 1852, began:

"In approaching this subject, we shall do well to remember that the Scriptures were never intended to be a scientific manual; that they speak of the phenomena of Nature in language which, although not scientifically correct, is understood and received among us without misleading anyone. . . .

The earth is the laboratory of the Deity, in which for thousands of years He carried on operations, preparing it gradually for higher and higher developments of organic life."

There were a number of magazines with a predominantly religious emphasis, like *The Christian Lady's Magazine*, edited by Charlotte Elizabeth Tonna, one of the most fervent of the early feminists. She wrote numerous articles urging women to inform themselves on questions of national interest, and she continually tried to stir the public conscience by publishing harrowing details of the lives of women and children in the factories.

Eliza Cook's Journal was an influential women's periodical of a more serious type. Issued in monthly parts, it supported every movement for social and political reform, every effort to raise the status of women and give them an education, every new inquiry into science and philosophy. It carried no fashion-plates, no gossip columns, no household hints, and preached no brand of religion except the necessity to tolerate every brand. The editorials and articles dealt with contemporary problems which were stimulating the reformers of the day: housing, the sweated industries, children's factory labour, ragged schools, public health and hygiene. There were book reviews and accounts of foreign travel and customs, but the main appeal of the journal was directed towards the early Victorian woman who wanted to know what was happening in the world which lay beyond her well-cushioned home.

Sport for women, as we know it, did not play any part in the leisure hours of a girl a hundred years ago; she would have thought of an 'athletic woman' with horror. But the early Victorian miss or matron of an energetic temperament managed to get a surprising amount of exercise.

Riding was the most usual form it took; it was not a very expensive pursuit, and there were parks in the cities, and country lanes and fields on the outskirts of towns, where horses could canter without distraction. Queen Victoria was a good horsewoman, and during her early and middle years could be seen riding in Windsor Park or at Balmoral.

Women rode side-saddle, and their riding-habits, though graceful, were the reverse of practical. The close-fitting bodice had long, tight sleeves, and the skirt was so voluminous that it was dangerous to the rider if she took a fall, for it was liable to get entangled in the stirrups and drag her along the ground. A man's top-hat, unblocked, draped with a veil, was the usual headgear until the forties, when a soft felt hat trimmed with a feather gave the wearer a more feminine look.

The game of croquet, which we think of as the arch-Victorian sport for ladies, did not reach its great vogue until the sixties and later; but in a story published in 1850 there is a reference to a young woman who took all eyes at afternoon parties because "she played a fierce game of croquet."

Skating was popular throughout the century, and the fact that ice could be artificially manufactured made the sport possible in summer as well as in winter. A writer in *The Ladies' Treasury* remarks:

"Skating makes a useful addition to our modes of exercise and recreation. It is as good for girls as it is for young men. If they do not learn quite so quickly, they make up by greater ultimate proficiency and grace. Without denying that a little of the attractiveness of skating is due to opportunities it affords of a little quiet flirtation, it deserves support as a means of exercise and a stimulus to active locomotion."

Leech's drawings of young women energetically rowing on a river indicate that many layers of petticoats did not deter the early Victorian maiden from strenuous exercise in boats.

Skittles, or ninepins, was another popular pastime, as was Aunt Sally. A Leech drawing shows the latter game being played in a garden, where a girl, crinolined and neatly booted, is gathering together the sticks which had been shied at a black-faced wooden head.

The most elegant sport of the period was archery, popular for "its eminent gracefulness, and for its being adapted to every age and every degree of strength, for by altering the strength of the bows it may be practised from childhood to green old age." Archery meetings were a favourite social event, and were as much enjoyed by the spectators as by the participants. An opera-dancer of the period observed that of all the attitudes she ever studied not one was so graceful or displayed the form to better advantage than that of drawing the long bow. The archer stood sideways to the target, and the effect of drawing the bow was to make her hold herself erect with her shoulders back, and her arm flexed to the shape of a bird's wing.

The observer looked for grace, and it was this physical attribute which distinguished the early Victorian sportswoman. Straight-backed old ladies in the later decades of the century, watching their granddaughters develop a fine muscular forearm at lawn tennis, may have thought with nostalgia of themselves when young—poised, bow drawn to shoulder, dressed in a velvet jacket braided and buttoned, a *gilet* and undersleeves of silk fluttering white in the breeze, a feathered hat of beaver, and kid boots which had 'chanelled' cork soles to guard their feet from the dew.

IX

AMUSEMENTS

Opera and Ballet—Balls, Soirées, Lectures—Panoramas, Dioramas, Cos-moramas—Street Peepshows—Amusement Gardens: Regent's Park, Vaux-hall Gardens, Cremorne Gardens—Theatres—Concerts

FOR those of us who wonder how people amused them-selves before the days of the cinema and mass sports meetings a glance at the advertisements of any nine-teenth-century newspaper is illuminating. The Victorians entertained themselves very well, and it is clear that there was plenty to amuse them in the thirties and forties.

They liked going to the theatre, to the opera, and ballet; they liked great spectacular shows, and firework displays, and public balls, and soirées of all kinds. They crowded to hear travellers tell of far-off lands, and found lantern lectures as enthralling as their descendants were to find moving pictures. The fact that they liked, when possible, to com-bine instruction with entertainment might indicate that they preferred something for their minds to bite on, even in their relaxation.

A strong appeal was always made to entertaining the family as a unit, hence the great popularity of panoramas, dioramas, and cosmoramas, which could be enjoyed by parents and children together. The panorama was a series of large pictures painted on canvas and exhibited in a hall, where it was slowly unrolled before the audience. Some-times the canvas was stretched round the inside of a circular building, and the spectators could ascend a winding stair-case to a platform in the centre of the rotunda, and examine the panorama from a height. The best-known places in London for seeing this kind of panorama were the Alhambra in Leicester Square, and the Colosseum in Regent's Park—the latter a pleasure resort which was demolished later in the century. There were panoramas on show in other parts of London, for, according to one chronicler:

"Never before have there existed such facilities for inspecting the wonders of the world by the aid of the painter and geographer as now abound in the Metropolis. The Panorama places before your eyes the architecture of great cities, the routes of nations, the haunts of tourists, and the seats of empires. Here is the Panorama of Europe from Dover to Constantinople. There is the Mediterranean, the Desert, New Zealand, the Arctic Regions . . . the Holy Land . . . the Falls of Niagara."

The panoramas were well painted in perspective, and a good deal of ingenuity went into the effects. At the evening exhibition of the "new and extraordinary panorama of London by night" there were atmospheric effects every half-hour, clouds passing over the moon and stars, and planets gleaming in the right places.

There was also the Diorama in Regent's Park; the building still exists in Park Square East. A diorama was an elaborate form of panorama. By the use of transparent sections in the scene and a clever arrangement of lights, changing views could be obtained. These shows were sometimes called dissolving views. A child of ten who saw one of them in 1840 wrote fifty years later: "I can still recollect the feeling of awe and wonder as I watched a storm over the painted mountains give way to sunshine."

The cosmorama was a kind of peepshow, a collection of scenes arranged in such a way as to be reflected from mirrors. It was looked at through a lens, which gave the spectator the sensation of gazing into a miniature world of three dimensions. Portable cosmoramas, or street peepshows, were the delight of children. They were taken round on a donkey-cart, with the owner acting as showman and his wife as helper. A small pair of steps was carried on the cart, and when the showman came to a good pitch he would let down the steps, and his wife would cry out to the children to bring up their pennies. Soon there would be a line of

CREMORNE GARDENS

From an engraving by J. Shury

By courtesy of the Director of the Victoria and Albert Museum

THE COLOSSEUM, REGENT'S PARK

From an engraving by T. Higham

By courtesy of the Trustees of the British Museum

96

CREMORNE GARDENS IN THE HEIGHT OF THE SEASON

William McConnell

boys and girls waiting their turn to mount the steps and look through the eyepiece at the brightly coloured scenes inside. It might be some recent national event, like the young Queen's coronation, or a wedding procession, or a first journey in a railway train. Or it might be something "wunnerful horrible," such as a representation of some notorious crime and its appropriate punishment.

The amusement gardens had sideshows of cosmoramas, together with life-size automata and other mechanical wonders. The show-piece in Regent's Park in the early forties was the Glacarium, the latest invention:

"We shall soon be independent altogether of climate or seasons. In this age of forcing we already have summer flowers in the winter, green peas with our ducks at Christmas, and now skating has actually become prevalent in July! By a combination of sodas, reduced to a liquid state by fusion, Mr Kirk, the inventor, has been enabled to produce artificial ice. When this new species of soda-water is poured upon the place destined to receive it the process of crystallization supervenes in less than half an hour, and skating may commence."

Admission to the Glacarium was included in the usual fee for the Colosseum, but should the onlooker wish to skate a moderate sum was asked for the privilege. "Chaste music" was later added to the attraction, and the admission fee was raised by sixpence.

Vauxhall Gardens and Cremorne Gardens, which had flourished under the Regency, were still popular, and constantly changed their programmes in order to attract clients. Vauxhall offered a Grand Scottish Fête, complete with chieftains in full Highland costume, pipers, songs, and dances: suitable family entertainment. But a few weeks later "the first Masquerade of the Season" was obviously intended for adults only. An account of this event gave a hint of the not-so-respectable reputation which these amusement gardens had inherited from wilder days:

"The quadrille bands played all the evening, and their exertions were well responded to by the dancers, who kept up the quadrilles and polkas with good-humoured spirit

G

until after daylight. It is something to say that up to this period nothing like a 'row' occurred to upset the general hilarity of the evening, and by those who recollect the scenes of dreary brutality presented by the masquerades half a dozen years back the advantage of this change will be readily acknowledged."

Cremorne offered a "never-ceasing round of amusements." There was a miniature zoo of monkeys, dogs, and goats, a giant ox, Tom Thumb's Fairy Cow, and "no end of fireworks by Mortman, the pyrotechnic Magician." A maze, an illuminated Arcadian Grove, a Swiss Cottage, pagoda orchestra, and monster platform for dancing were further enticements. No charge was made for admission, but every visitor was expected to take a refreshment card to the amount of sixpence. It was only when something very special was offered that a charge was made—for instance, when, in July 1848, Lieutenant Gale made his first night ascent in a balloon and discharged from mid-air a magnificent *feu d'artifice*. That cost each spectator a shilling, and the groups watching must have felt that it was well worth the money.

The theatre was immensely popular with all classes. There was the Theatre Royal, in Drury Lane, and Covent Garden opposite, the only two theatres which had royal patents and were officially allowed to perform plays. There were also about sixty minor theatres in London in the eighteen-forties, most of which evaded the patent laws by introducing music and miming into their plays. Theatres like Sadler's Wells put on tremendous water spectacles, Astley's gave entertainments on a grand scale in a circus arena, and Madame Vestris made her Olympic Theatre a centre of gaiety with her extravaganzas.

A family evening at the theatre did not cost a great deal; and it *was* an evening, for the performance began at seven o'clock or before and went on until midnight. A seat in a family box cost about five shillings; and there were plenty of boxes, for they extended right round the house on both main tiers.

There was usually a full-length piece, Shakespeare or another classical author; then a burlesque, a melodrama, and a short farcical entertainment to send the audience home in good spirits. If it were a pantomime the end-piece would be a harlequinade. F. C. Burnand, the Victorian humorist, has left a delightful description of the impressions made on him by his first pantomime, which he saw at the age of six, in 1842:

"I can recall that green baize curtain covering the stage. There began in the dress-circle a feverish peeling and rapid suction of refreshing oranges as little boys and girls . . . removed their white cotton gloves or mittens. . . . We had one eye fixed on the green curtain lest in a sudden moment of inattention on our parts it should go up suddenly and deprive us of seeing the very first, and, therefore, vitally important part of the pantomime.

"A sharp tap on his desk, given by the conductor of the orchestra, calls every one to order. In a second there is a hush! a silence! And then, O glorious moment in the Christmas life of a town-bred child, the overture of the panto-mime commences! What overture can ever equal a first-rate overture to a pantomime on the first night of perform-ance! What drawings-in of breath! fine parts for the deep bass of the brass cymbals, and drums of all sorts and sizes. Crash! Bang! The green curtain has long disappeared, and oh, joy, came the good fairies, the sprites—and soon we were roaring with laughter at the Clown, and were join-ing the audience in the uproarious demand for another song. The whacking, the banging, the horseplay, the tom-foolery of the comic scenes! We gloried in the Harlequin, loved the Columbine to desperation, loved the Clown, and were quite ready to laugh at the poor old doting Pantaloon."

Some of the smaller theatres specialized in burlettas and farces. Punning was the chief form of wit in these, and the appeal was simple and unsophisticated. It was topical too. In the autumn of 1851, when interest was still running high in the attempt to introduce Mrs Bloomer's trousered cos-tume for women, there appeared a current playbill:

TWO BLOOMERS

An Extra-extravaganzic Piece de Circonstance
dexterously handled, exhibiting and portraying
the Costume of the Coming Age and
Extravagances of the Present.

There was also a vogue for dramatized Dickens—mostly
without that author's permission, as he complained so often.
Scenes from *Oliver Twist, Nicholas Nickleby, David Copper-
field, The Chimes*, and others of his novels were pirated and
turned into stage-plays, and were always a great draw.

Another form of entertainment which drew the crowd in
the forties and fifties was opera. It was a period of great
singers—Jenny Lind and Castellan—who were talked of
in taverns as well as in drawing-rooms. The middle-class
woman was escorted in comfort to the opera; driven in a
carriage—her own or hired—and settled with fan and
flowers in the 'place' which had been reserved for her.
Those on a lower social plane were equally fond of this
sumptuous form of entertainment, and filled the cheaper
seats. Here is an extract from an account of a visit to the
opera by some one who could not afford the best places:

"You step out of the noise and bustle of the Haymarket
into Her Majesty's Opera House. If you have taken your
stand at the pit-door you will find many persons there before
you, and by the time the doors are opened you are jammed
in by a dense crowd. . . . Be thankful if you find your coat-
tails still behind you, or that your fair companion carries
with her the full complement of lace. . . .

"But it is at the gallery door that the terrific squeeze is to
be experienced in all its horrors. There is a surging of the
pent-up bodies, a rush from the impatient mass behind, and
many 'Oh! Oh's!' from the tender and bulky. . . . Slowly,
inch by inch, the *Pay Here* is reached, the long stair ascended,
and you are seated, spent and gasping, far aloft in the
magnificent theatre, on a level with the great chandelier, and
see below you, a great way off, the splendid proscenium and
the footlights in the still dimly-lighted orchestra. The

boxes are hung with draperies of marigold satin . . . bright faces of beautiful women beam from them . . . there are generals, members of Parliament, dukes; and lo! there is the Queen and Royal Family in that box, the third from the stage. And now the full gas is put on and the house is lit up in a blaze of splendour."

Concerts were less formal occasions, except, of course, when stars of the magnitude of Jenny Lind crowded the Hanover Street Rooms or one of the assembly halls. The Swedish Nightingale was one of the idols of the musical public, and her appearances in London were eagerly talked of.

The lesser occasions were well supported too, and there are notices in most of the women's journals of *Soirées classiques* and musical matinées, "well attended by an elegant female audience." Vocal concerts were especially crowded, for besides the pleasure of hearing songs correctly sung, it was useful to know of new ones for one's daughters to sing at home. Amateur singing being an important part of social life, the early Victorian woman patronized every occasion which would allow her to hear the best which the professionals had to offer.

X

HOLIDAYS AND TRAVEL

The Family Seaside Holiday—The Expansion of Railway Travel—Hotels and Boarding-houses—Lodgings—Mrs Carlyle finds Bugs—Seaside Occupations—Trippers—The Beginnings of Excursions—Travelling abroad—Noted Women Travellers

THE family seaside holiday, as part of the accepted pattern of life, began in the early Victorian period. Before then only the comparatively wealthy took holidays, travelling to the country or to the fashionable spas in their own carriages. But their numbers were small, and the resorts which they patronized catered for visitors with an expensive standard of living.

The coming of the railways, in the eighteen-thirties, brought a great change. From the beginning railway travel was cheap; the promotors of the new companies set out to appeal to the vast number of people in the prospering artisan and middle classes who would prove to be their steadiest customers. The wealthy could travel in puffily upholstered first-class carriages, and the less wealthy in a comfortable second-class; but there would also be plenty of accommodation in a third-class, even though the sides of the coaches were open to the weather above shoulder level.

By the middle of the forties the new railways had pushed fingers out to the coasts in all directions. The established resorts, like Scarborough, in the north, and Brighton, in the south, were building rows of apartment houses behind the Regency terraces and crescents on their sea-fronts. Villages all along the coasts which had formerly lived by fishing now decided that they were picturesque, and set out to attract holiday-makers.

The smaller towns in between the known resorts also saw the possibilities, and began to build piers and esplanades. They furbished up reading-rooms and circulating libraries, and allowed private speculators to put up lines of houses for letting as lodgings, no matter how inharmonious these were against the native background. Branch-lines from the main railway were considered the greatest asset to these aspiring holiday towns, and where there was no railway, coaches were provided to ply between the town and the nearest station.

By the early eighteen-fifties the summer holiday by the sea was firmly established. Queen Victoria bought a house at Osborne, in the Isle of Wight, in 1845, and her children played on the sands. "Wherever the people in high life take a lead, the next class eagerly follow," and the royal example brought an evergrowing number of families to the seaside every year. The Queen had shown that she approved of railway travel, in spite of the disquieting number of accidents reported in the newspapers every week. The public was glad of cheap transport, but there was still an element of danger in these strange marvels of steam carriages. The loyal tradesman in a town which was getting ready for a royal visit must have felt this doubt when he inscribed on a banner outside his shop:

Hail to Prince Albert, the pride of the nation!
May his journey be safe when he goes from the station.[1]

The railways were developing at such a rate, however, that it was difficult not to have confidence in them, and, though stage-coaches continued to run to many of the coast resorts up to the late forties, the trains got most of the custom.

There was soon a wide choice of holiday places for the Victorian mother to consider. In the north, Whitby was becoming known, and Blackpool, on the west coast, was already making a name for itself among the Lancashire manufacturers. The Welsh coast-towns began to advertise in the newspapers and railway guides, Aberystwyth and

[1] Lady Dorothy Nevill, *Under Five Reigns.*

Tenby being particularly forward. The South Devon coast opened up with Torquay, Sidmouth, and Teignmouth, and Lyme Regis began to extend, too, in a modest way, knowing herself to be as securely established as Weymouth, farther along the seaboard.

Families from London went to Brighton or to the newer resorts along the Sussex and Kentish coasts. The "marine village of Broadstairs" offered quietness and comfort, in contrast to Southend, which aimed at being "a place of recreation and resort to a portion of the population of the metropolis," and frankly set out to be cheap and cheerful.

The Victorian mother who took her family to the sea could not do so with a carefree mind. She was only able to relax when she arrived there and found that the rooms which she had engaged did not fall too far short of their promise. Advertisements offered so much: spacious rooms, the best cooking, the most devoted service, the lowest charges. The reality was too often a disappointment. There were few hotels and boarding-houses at the resorts; most families took lodgings and bought their own food, which was cooked by the landlady. This system had its trials. Landladies were notoriously dishonest, and the mother of a family had to count her stores daily. Entries in diaries throw up this harassing side of a seaside holiday a century ago: "We should be tolerably comfortable here, save that Mrs T— is undoubtedly cutting at our ham."

The hotels and boarding-houses provided food, but raised their prices out of all reason during July and August, giving little in return for their high charges. Jane Welsh Carlyle, writing to her husband from Ryde in August 1843, says:

"We reached Ryde at eight o'clock in the evening, and, the second hotel being filled, had to take up our quarters for that night at the first, which is 'the dearest hotel in Europe,' and the hotel in Europe, so far as I have seen, where there is the least human comfort. I had to make tea from an urn, the water of which was certainly not 'as hot as one can drink it'; and the cream was blue milk, the butter tasted of straw, and the cold fowl was a lukewarm one, and as tough as leather."

She left that hotel for lodgings, but the following morning she wrote again to Carlyle, complaining of what was not an unusual phenomenon in hired rooms at holiday resorts: "No doubt about it, I have fallen among bugs! My neck was all bitten infamously." Two days later:

"I have not for a long time enjoyed a more triumphant moment than in descending from the railway yesterday at Vauxhall, and calling a porter to carry my small trunk and dressing-box to a Chelsea steamer. To be sure I looked and felt as if just returning from the Thirty Years War. Sleepless, bug-bitten, bedusted, and bedevilled, I was hardly recognizable for the same trim little Goody who had left that spot only four days before. . . . A few minutes more, and I should be purified to the shift—should have absolutely bathed myself with eau de Cologne."

Bugs were taken for granted to quite an astonishing degree by landladies and hotel-keepers, whose attitude generally was that livestock of this order was inevitable with changing lodgers, and the clients must protect themselves as best they could.

Sedateness was the keynote of the early Victorian scene at the seaside. The atmosphere had changed entirely from that of twenty or thirty years before, when the visitors had been lively beaux and belles who danced at the Assembly Rooms, drank the waters at the Pump Room, and took coffee in the circulating library. These buildings still remained, but the gaiety had departed. The only link between the two eras was the bathing-machine, which had come into use at the end of the eighteenth century, and was now an essential part of the bathing ritual.

Bathing in the sea was still a medicinal rite, as it had been in earlier years. One went down to the beach in the very early morning and engaged a bathing-machine—a hut on wheels, drawn by a horse. One changed into an enveloping costume while being trundled over the sand and shingle to the sea edge. A canvas awning was then let down from the hut-roof, and one was dipped up and down in the waves by a bathing-woman with bare legs and doubled-up skirts. Then back to civilization, drying and changing on the way, thankful that the bathe was over.

The rest of the day was filled in with walks along the shore, collecting shells and seaweed, classifying seaside flora, and, above all, sketching in water-colours and reading. Scores of the cartoons of the period show young ladies, fully clad in the current fashion, sitting on rocks sketching or reading. They had little else to do. The Assembly Rooms, where formerly a Master of Ceremonies introduced strangers to each other, now provided concerts and lectures, and the etiquette which governed the making of acquaintanceships at home was just as strong here.

There were donkey-rides for children on the sands, but no games, no sports, for those who were growing up. The family group was static, and usually complete. The early Victorian family took its holiday as a unit, sufficient unto itself, inexorably genteel. It was the swing of the pendulum right away from the freedom and easiness of behaviour which had characterized the seaside of the Regency.

A new visitor began to appear at Margate, Ramsgate, and Southend: the day-tripper. The rise of the tripper was the direct outcome of cheap means of travel, both on the railways and the pleasure steamers which took thousands of Londoners down the Thames Estuary and round the coast of Thanet. Whether they went for the day or a week-end or a week, they were still essentially trippers—out to make a cheerful noise, to put their hard-working lives behind them and fill the all-too-short hours of leisure full to bursting with jollity.

The contemporary cartoons in *Punch* and the accounts of seaside trippers in the forties and fifties warm the heart even now. They *enjoyed* themselves so unashamedly. They saved all the year round for this annual beanfeast, and then poured out their savings in a riot of high spirits. The early Victorian working-woman was well to the fore in this sunlit scene on Ramsgate sands; sempstress and shop-woman, labourer's wife and artisan's daughter, she let her back hair down in more senses than one, and joined her menfolk in a holiday mood which was the reverse of genteel.

They spread themselves on the beach, picnicking on shrimps and oysters and fried fish, on eels and bloaters and cold beef and steak-pies. They listened to troupes of nigger minstrels singing strange songs from far-off America; they gave coppers to the cornet-players and German bands who added to the pandemonium. Noise and food and laughter: the tripper's holiday was not refined, but it was intensely alive.

There was a more serious type of tripper in the North, where Thomas Cook, the secretary of a temperance association and a young man of vision and energy, was beginning an experiment which was to lead in later years to an enormous tourist industry. Cook did not begin his career with that aim in view. In the summer of 1841 he wanted to get as many people as possible from Leicester to a temperance demonstration in another town, and arranged with the railway company to put on an extra long train at a moderate return fare. Most of the railways already ran excursions, but the success of the temperance excursion made Cook realize that this system could be extended. He believed in travel as a means of education, and he saw that the railways could enable the mass of working-people to get away for a time from their grey surroundings, and so, he hoped, enlarge their minds.

Cook began to put his ideas into practical effect. He persuaded working-men to save for holidays through their clubs; their response was immediate and encouraging, and Cook had the satisfaction of knowing that money that might have been spent on drink was being saved for a good purpose. The railway companies were only too glad to co-operate with him, and more and more excursions appeared on the schedules. An article in *Eliza Cook's Journal* gives a long description of the excursionist, remarking:

"The Tripper is the growth of railways and monster trains. Before they were, he was not. Tens of thousands of operatives formerly grew old who had never seen the sea. The operative and his family were then restricted to the dingy localities where they lived, and rarely escaped from beyond the sound of spindles and power looms. . . . Now they collect into trains of from one to two thousand passengers, sometimes to cathedral towns, often to London itself, but oftenest of all to the seashore."

In 1851 Cook ran excursions to London for the Great Exhibition, and in 1855 he launched out more ambitiously and arranged excursions to the Paris Exhibition. He paid attention to all the details of travel and to the comfort of the passengers in his charge. The venture was such a success that he proceeded with plans for further travel on the Continent.

Travelling abroad was well established by the forties. Switzerland had been popular since the beginning of the century, though it was always considered expensive. France and Germany were more within the means of the average middle-class family, especially after the Continental railways had connected the Channel ports with inland resorts like Aix-les-Bains, Avignon, Wiesbaden, and the rest. Branch-lines, however, were few, and the English family who wanted to see life abroad as it was lived in small towns and villages had to travel by diligence, a public carriage of the stage-coach type.

Lady Dorothy Nevill, a noted traveller of Victorian days, gives a charming account of one of her journeys on the Continent in the forties:

"You saw the country through which you passed in its everyday, natural state, the people living their own lives in repose, unspoilt as yet by a constantly moving herd of travellers. Everything then seemed full of its own identity. For the most part, the peasantry in the country districts were honest and simple, very religious and very fond of their local traditions. The table d'hôte—now everywhere a copy of a pretentious meal—was literally what it professed to be; the master of the house presided, gave you the best he had, and told you all the news of the country round."[1]

Lady Dorothy was an experienced traveller, and her

[1] Lady Dorothy Nevill, *Under Five Reigns.*

wealth and position made things comparatively easy, especially as she was suitably escorted. It was very different when Barbara Leigh Smith and her friend Bessie Parkes went off on a tour of Belgium, Germany, Austria, and Switzerland in 1850. Barbara was twenty-three, Bessie was twenty-one; they had no chaperon, and they had never been abroad before. It was a daring and adventurous thing for them to do, but their enthusiasm was not damped by the conventions. Young women were reaching out for wider horizons, and Benjamin Leigh Smith trusted his daughter's common sense.

Barbara's travels through Continental countries which had only recently been in a state of revolutionary ferment showed her at first hand what political tyranny meant. She was oppressed by the sight of so many armed soldiers in the German states and in Austria—"the sight of the people ruled by the sword in place of law would stir up my heart, and make me feel as miserable as those who live under it."

Of the early Victorian women travellers who made journeys far overseas and wrote books about their travels, Julia Pardoe was one of the best known in her own day. In her later years she published novels, but these are not nearly so interesting as the accounts she wrote of her journeys in Turkey, Portugal, and Hungary. She was born in 1806, and when she was still a girl she accompanied her father to Turkey, where he had a diplomatic appointment. Julia was naturally lively and curious. In *The Beauties of the Bosphorus* she gives realistic descriptions of the domestic life of Turkish women, as well as of ceremonial occasions in the fabulous towns of the Sultan's kingdom. She visited the Valley of Sweet Waters, where she noted "the bullock carriages, covered with gay-coloured awnings of silken shag, fringed with gold." She was allowed into the women's quarters, and became friends with several Turkish ladies who allowed her to accompany them to the baths, of which she says:

"The bath is the very paradise of Eastern women. Here they assemble to discuss every subject of interest and amusement, whether politics, scandal, or news; to arrange marriages, and to prevent them; to display their domestic supremacy and to impart their domestic grievances; but, above all, to enjoy the noise, the hurry, the excitement, which form so great a contrast to the calm and monotony of the harem."

Lady Emmeline Stuart Wortley was another traveller who ranged over half the world with a matter-of-factness and indifference to discomfort which were the admiration of her contemporaries. In 1849, left a widow, she took her young daughter as companion and went to America, deciding to travel on that continent. She saw Niagara, turned south and travelled over the Alleghenies, and reached the Isthmus of Panama by way of Mexico. She went what would now be called the 'hard' way, taking whatever transport was available, herself dealing with rascally couriers and thieving landlords of inns, eating strange dishes, and living at times in primitive conditions which would have been inconceivable to her friends at home. Returning to England after seeing more of the North and South American continent than any Englishwoman before her, she set out again on her travels in 1851.

This time she took a route through Spain, Portugal, and Morocco, observing the life and customs of the people, and avoiding the usual track of travellers. She was away for a year, and in 1855 set off yet once again on what proved to be her last journey. She went to Constantinople and the Near East, travelling through Cairo, Jerusalem, and Damascus; she was taken ill in the desert, and died in her daughter's arms. The girl, grief-stricken as she was, was able to seek the necessary help in the circumstances—surely one of the strangest tasks that ever fell to the lot of a girl still in her teens.

A very different traveller in the East was Emily Eden, a daughter of the first Lord Auckland. She began, in fact, by being an unwilling traveller, for she would not have chosen to spend so many years of her middle life away from England; she was forced by circumstances to be an exile. Her father had been Ambassador to many courts. Her mother had had a child in every country to which they had been sent, and had written in her diary: "Out of fourteen I suckled thirteen. Eleven of the children had smallpox during their wanderings, also cow-pox, whooping-cough, measles, and scarlet fever."

Emily was used to the idea of foreign travel and its hazards, though she had been thankful when her parents had at last returned to England and settled down to make a permanent home. After their deaths she and her younger sister, Fanny—the only two unmarried daughters—lived with George, their eldest brother, who was also unmarried and had succeeded his father as the second Lord Auckland. He was appointed Governor-General of India in 1835, and asked Emily and Fanny to accompany him to India.

Emily was now thirty-eight years old, happy with many sisters and their families to visit, and with varied interests to keep her occupied. The prospect of a five months' sea-voyage was not inviting, and she was sad at the thought of leaving her home and relations, to whom she was much attached. But her brother needed a hostess for official occasions in India, and Emily Eden, like so many of her generation, had a strong sense of duty; besides which, she and Fanny were devoted to George. In September 1835 they sailed with him to India.

They were away until 1842, and during their many journeys in India they both kept up a large correspondence with their sisters and intimate friends. In later life Emily became known as a novelist, the author of *The Semi-Attached Couple* and *The Semi-Detached House*, but she was at her best in her letters home. She was a born descriptive writer, intelligent and politically perceptive, with an occasional tart pen which was balanced by a warm heart. She was also an artist of some talent, and her accounts of personalities and ceremonies give an instant picture of a scene through visual impressions:

"We drove for two miles and a half through a lane of Runjeet's 'goocherras,' or bodyguard. The sun was up and shining on them . . . one troop was dressed entirely in yellow satin, with gold scarfs and shawls; but the other half were in that cloth of gold which is called kincob—the *fond* being gold and the pattern scarlet, or purple, or yellow; their arms were all gold—many of them had collars of precious stones; their shields and lances were all studded with gold. They have long beards down to their waists, and most of them had a silver or gold tissue drapery, which they bring over their heads and pass round their beards to protect them from the dust."

Here is another scene:

"I suppose fifty horses were led past us. The first had on its emerald trappings, necklaces arranged on its neck and between its ears, and in front of the saddle two enormous emeralds, nearly two inches square, carved all over and set in gold frames, like little looking-glasses. The crupper was all emeralds, and there were stud-ropes of gold put on something like a martingale. . . . The next horse was simply attired in diamonds and turquoises, another in pearls, and there was one with trappings of coral and pearl that was very pretty."

But she had a quick eye for more than magnificence. She and her sister, with their entourage, accompanied George on his State journeys, and Emily thought a great deal about this recently conquered country. She wrote from Simla:

"Twenty years ago no European had ever been here, and there we were [last night] with the band playing . . . and eating salmon from Scotland and sardines from the Mediterranean . . . and observing . . . that some of the ladies' sleeves were too tight . . . and all this in the face of those high hills, some of which have remained untrodden since the creation, and we 105 Europeans being surrounded by at least 3000 mountaineers, who, wrapped up in their hill blankets, looked on at what we call our polite amusements, and bowed to the ground if a European came near them. I sometimes wonder they do not all cut our heads off, and say nothing more about it."

Life was not always as comfortable as at Simla. She travelled for weeks over the hot plains, on horseback or sitting in a palanquin, camping at night and catching agues through getting constantly wet—"The pleasure of walking along a hard floor [again] . . . without hearing the ground

THE FAIR TOXOPHILITES

CONSTANCE : Oh, Mama ! I'm so delighted. I've just made the best Gold, and won the beautiful bracelet given by Captain Rifles.
LUCY (disappointed) : Well, Constance, I think you had better not say much about it. You know it was a Fluke, for you told me that you always shot with your eyes shut, as you feel so nervous !

From a coloured lithograph after J. Leech

By courtesy of Mrs Bernard Croft-Murray.

SKATING

From a lithograph in the Cannan Collection

By courtesy of the Trustees of the British Museum

113

squelch!" She helped the villagers against petty oppressors, and bought two children who had been abandoned, sending them to school where she knew they would be kindly treated and settled in life.

Little escaped her—the delicate traceries of a ruined mosque or the discreet flirtations of her brother's aides with ladies of the party. But, with all her wit, she had a charity and tolerance of the weaknesses of human beings which make one like and admire her greatly across the span of a hundred years.

H

PART II

THE WORLD OUTSIDE THE HOME

XI

WOMEN WRITERS

A 'Respectable Occupation'—Hostility against Female Authors—Fashionable Writers—The Moralists—Circulating Libraries—The Romance Writers—The Novel-with-a-purpose—The Great Writers

IT is a measure of the quality of the greatest of the Victorian women novelists that they are not thought of by our generation as 'women novelists,' but as major writers of the nineteenth century. Their contemporaries were not so objective. In spite of the fact that writing books was a respectable occupation for women, and 'authoresses' were welcomed by publishers and highly thought of by the public in general, the Brontës felt that they had to adopt masculine names to prevent prejudice, and Mary Ann Evans published all her books save one under the name of George Eliot.

Outside the foremost literary men of the day, who accepted women writers of their own standard without question, there was plenty of hostility against them, sometimes from other women. It might be summed up in the attitude of Miss M. A. Stodart, who wrote a book called *Female Writers: Thoughts on Their Proper Sphere*. That sphere, she pointed out, was not one in which books should be written. If women must have learning let them study Latin and Greek for their own edification—preferably when employed upon some useful needlework. But let them not have the vanity to transmute their learning into creative literature.

Miss Stodart was frank about the reasons behind her strictures:

"It is—why should we veil the truth?—a dislike to talent in general, to female talent in particular. Pride, though not made for man, is natural to man; few like to acknowledge, even to feel, that others are superior to themselves. . . . This hatred of superiority in general blazes with particular fury against anything of intellectual superiority in the weaker sex. Argue as you will, it is the fact; and the heat is not the less intense because the fire is concealed."

The Stodarts and their like did not discourage the growing numbers of women writers, many of whom made a good deal of money from their work; though there must have been many more who enriched their publishers out of all proportion, for women were miserably timid in money matters. Still, they made a livelihood. Miss Mitford supported a feckless father for many years, Felicia Hemans educated five sons on her earnings, and Frances Trollope saved her family from near-destitution by beginning to write at the age of fifty and keeping up a regular output of books for many years.

There was a great deal published by women; on the shelves of antiquarian bookshops one finds rows of novels, historical romances, and volumes of poems which were successes for a few years, but which have never been heard of since. The books which have survived have become classics, and it is a little startling to read contemporary reviews of these works which give no indication of their future fame. The books which to us are classics were part of the large output of the period.

The leisured woman changed her novels frequently at the circulating library; she must have been a rapid reader, for most novels were very long. There was much discreet publicity in the popular journals about 'female authors,' with emphasis on their habits of industry and blameless private lives. It was, however, accepted that lady authors on the higher levels of society had less strict standards.

The Countess of Blessington was constantly before the public from 1830 to 1850, both as an editor of the fashionable Annuals and as a novelist. An Irish beauty with a romantic and faintly scandalous past, she had been a belle

of the Regency, and was a close friend of the elegant and
dissipated Court d'Orsay. They were both continually in
need of money, and Lady Blessington capitalized her early
friendship with Lord Byron in a book which was immediately successful: *Conversations with Byron*. There followed
stories contributed to the Annuals and magazines, and more
novels, which sold well, but which had a mixed reception
from the critics. Charles Greville, writing in his *Journal* in
February 1839, made this biting comment:

"*Lady Blessington*. The fact of her existence as an
authoress is an enigma, poor as her pretensions are; for
while it is very difficult to write good books, it is not easy
to compose even bad ones, and volumes have come forth
under her name for which hundreds of pounds have been
paid because (Heaven only can tell how) thousands are
found who will read them. Her 'works' have been published in America . . . where they seem to have met with
big successes; and this trash goes down because it is written
by a Countess, in a country where rank is eschewed, and
equality is the universal passion. . . . I never met with any
individual who had read any of her books, except the *Conversations with Byron*, which are too good to be hers. They
are unquestionably a source of considerable profit, and she
takes her place confidently and complacently as one of the
literary celebrities of the day."

Caroline Norton was another writer of the 'high life'
school, and though she did not make so much money as
did Lady Blessington, she earned a good income by her
romantic tales.

A far more acute and satiric observer of the social scene
was Catherine Frances Gore, who was popular for many
years. She published her first novel in 1824, when she was
in her twenties, and by the time failing eyesight forced her
to retire, in 1850, she had written about seventy novels and
many volumes of plays and poems. The quality of her work
was uneven, but she had abundant wit, grace, and good
humour, and though she used a fine blade to prick snobbery
and pretension, the point was never tipped with malice.
Mrs Gore's novels were about people in the world of fashion,

and as she ridiculed that world, she delighted both the cynics and the middle-class readers, who had not yet climbed into the regions above them. In one of her sketches of society life she gave John Bull a glimpse of his attitude towards women:

"For John adores woman in the singular, and hates her in the plural; John loves, but does not like. Woman is the object of his passion, rarely of his regard. There is nothing in the gaiety of heart or sprightliness of intellect of the weaker sex which he considers an addition to society. To him, women are an interruption to business and pleasure."

Mrs Gore would have been a success in any era: her thrusts would have delighted the eighteenth century as well as the twentieth. Maria Edgeworth, on the other hand, was the progenitor of a peculiarly Victorian institution—the moral tale. Miss Edgeworth was already a long-established writer by the thirties and forties. She was born in 1767, and her best-known book, *Castle Rackrent*, was published in 1800. She went on writing to within a few years of her death, in 1849, and during our period she was an institution, a link with the great figures of the preceding decades, for she had been a friend of Scott, who admired her work.

If one adds uplift and religion to the moral tone Charlotte Mary Yonge was the most esteemed authoress of the Edgeworth school, though she lacked the Irish writer's liveliness and flashes of humour. She made up for these qualities in earnestness and zeal, and her Victorian readers responded to her obvious sincerity by making her into a best-seller.

Charlotte Yonge was born in Hampshire in 1823, and was brought up in an atmosphere of religious fervour. John Keble, one of the moving spirits of the Oxford Movement, lived in a neighbouring village, and Charlotte was strongly influenced by his High Church views. She began to write stories for a religious magazine while she was still a girl, and several books followed. Then, in 1853, she published the story that was to make her famous, *The Heir of Redclyffe*. It was the model moral story. Sir Guy Morville, the hero, was "right-minded," "very well informed," and noble to a degree. Amy, the heroine, was pure, gentle, womanly, and clinging, given to running to her mother to tell of everything that happened to her. The book held up an uncompromising ideal of what perfect domestic life should be, with every virtue neatly in place and an aura of High Church piety over all. It sold by the thousand.

Heartsease followed in 1854, and *The Daisy Chain* two years later. This last was almost as popular as *The Heir*, for Miss Yonge was able to give enough money to build a missionary college in New Zealand with the proceeds; she devoted all her earnings to missionary purposes. Charlotte Yonge died in 1901, the author of well over a hundred books, most of them written on the same pattern. As one reviewer said: "Miss Yonge's work can, with perfect propriety, be left open on the drawing-room table."

Miss Yonge had a tribe of imitators, though individual prejudices in religion varied the brands of piety. Elizabeth Sewell published *Amy Herbert* in 1844, and about forty further works of a High Church complexion. Anna Maria Hall wrote sketches and tales of Ireland, with a more evangelical bias: *The Worn Thimble, a Story of Woman's Duty and Woman's Influence*, in 1853, and *The Drunkard's Bible*, a year later.

Sarah Ellis—the Mrs Ellis of countless magazine articles —played safe, and concentrated on duties and responsibilities. Her strong point was general morality; the title of one of her books, *Prevention Better Than Cure, or The Moral Wants of the World We Live In*, was also her favourite theme.

Dinah Maria Mulock, who later became Mrs Craik, published her first novel, *The Ogilvies*, in 1849, when she was twenty-three. Three more books followed, then she wrote *John Halifax, Gentleman*, which came out in 1857 and was an immediate success. A West-country story of thrift, industry, and irreproachable morals, it was exactly to the taste of the middle-class patron of the circulating library.

Margaret Oliphant appealed to a more discriminating public than Mrs Craik. Her first book, *Margaret Maitland*, published in 1849, revealed a quiet, true talent for describing Scottish life, and she was recognized by her literary contemporaries as a writer of quality. She was a fertile author, and built up a reputation which reached fame in the sixties, when her *Chronicles of Carlingford* began to come out. From then until the end of her long life she was known as a most industrious writer; but some critics hinted that the high promise of her early work had been levelled to a competent mediocrity.

The greatest demand at the circulating libraries was for novels of romance, and there were many "females of fervent imagination," as one reviewer called them, to supply these stories. The circulating libraries were powerful arbiters of popular taste. Charles Edward Mudie, who opened his Select Library in 1842, really did insist on keeping it select, and propriety had to be a necessary ingredient in a novel, however romantic, if the book was to find a place on his shelves.

There was, for a time, a vogue for the tale of mystery and suspense, with a plot centred round an *ingénue* heroine— usually a governess—who found herself involved in some dark intrigue. Purity and innocence always triumphed over the powers of evil, and the story ended with a betrothal, or, quite as often, with the sinner repentant on his death-bed.

Echoes of the Gothic romances of former days were found in the ghost stories of Catherine Crowe, whose *Light and Darkness, or Mysteries of Life*, in 1850, and *Adventures of a Beauty*, in 1852, appealed to sensation-loving subscribers to the libraries. Caroline Clive wrote on a higher level; her *Paul Ferroll, a Tale*, published in 1855, was talked of for months, and she was also highly praised for her poetry, though some reviewers found her gloomy.

There was a spate of historical romances or novels with a foreign setting. Julia Pardoe published many novels in the forties and fifties with backgrounds based on her travels in Turkey and Hungary. Mary Howitt, well known through her journalism, made admirable translations from the Danish, including several of Hans Andersen's stories. She translated, edited, or wrote over a hundred works, including *Little Coin, Much Care*, 1842, and *No Sense Like Common Sense*, 1843—which give an indication of her favourite themes.

Eliza Lynn Linton began her long career with *Azeth the Egyptian*, in 1846, though it was not until much later in the century that she was to make a minor sensation with her *Saturday Review* essays, "The Girl of the Period." Catherine Sinclair hit the popular taste with *Modern Flirtations, or a Month at Harrowgate*, in 1841, and Geraldine Jewsbury— mentioned so often with irritation and affection by Mrs Carlyle—wrote six or seven novels which were in constant demand at the libraries in the forties. Anne Marsh was another authoress much asked for; she wrote over twenty romances, the best known being *Ravenscliffe*, which came out in 1851.

The most astonishing of these professional novelists was Frances Trollope. She did not begin writing for a living until she was well into middle life, and then she rushed into fame—and notoriety—with a book based on her impressions of America. She later turned to novel-writing with the energy and patience which had been her mainstay through a hard and chequered life, which had all the elements of a novel itself.

Born in 1780, Frances married at about the age of thirty, and had six children. Her husband was a clergyman and a scholar, but he was unable to support his family, and there was much hardship and poverty in the home. Anthony Trollope, in his *Autobiography*, has given a frank account of the miseries of his early years because of his father's inadequacies.

Frances grew tired of narrow means and creditors, and decided to go to America to establish a business; she felt there would be more scope in that country for her sons. The business failed, and she returned home; but she had watched life critically in the new world, and she wrote a book which she called *The Domestic Manners of the Americans*. It was published in 1832, and it infuriated the Americans, for Mrs Trollope had been unsparing in her opinions of their habits of thought as well as their manners. The book sold well, and Frances Trollope knew that she need endure poverty no more; she could write.

Book followed book with steady industry. Anthony

Trollope says little about the quality of his mother's work in the *Autobiography*, but he pays tribute to her toughness of character in keeping on with her work through months of anxiety and grief. His brother was consumptive, his father and younger sister were ill; Mrs Trollope nursed them all, and went on with her own work at the same time:

"There were two sick men in the house, and hers were the hands that tended them. The novels went on, of course. We had already learned to know that they would be forthcoming at stated intervals—and they were always forthcoming. The doctor's vials and the ink-bottle held equal places in my mother's room. . . . Her power of dividing herself into two parts, and keeping her intellect by itself clear from the troubles of the world, and fit for the duty it had to do, I never saw equalled. I do not think that the writing of a novel is the most difficult task which a man may be called upon to do; but it is a task that may be supposed to demand a spirit fairly at ease. The work of doing it with a troubled mind killed Sir Walter Scott. My mother went through it unscathed in strength, though she performed all the work of day-nurse and night-nurse to a sick household."

Frances Trollope was steadily successful with her novels, conventional as they were: *The Widow Barnaby* in 1838, *Young Love* in 1844, *The Young Countess, or Love and Jealousy* in 1848. One of her books, however, was praised as a contribution to the growing literature on social problems—her story of mill-life, *The Life and Adventures of Michael Armstrong, the Factory Boy*, published in 1840.

The mass of poetry which appeared in every magazine of the period, and in volume upon volume in the bookshops and libraries, shows that it was a popular form of literature. The experienced authoress of romances could usually turn out verses by the yard, and some writers wrote most of their work in the medium of the narrative poem.

Laetitia Elizabeth Landon—the "L.E.L." of the thirties —enjoyed a quite extraordinary devotion from a large public. She was born in 1802, and began to write verses in her early teens. Before she was twenty a publisher was paying her £300 for a narrative poem, *The Improvisatrice*, and

£600 for another, *The Troubadour*. Like so many other women writers of her time, she needed money to help support relations; she was, in the contemporary phrase, an "industrious writer." She had a capacity for hard work; she edited a Scrapbook for eight years, and wrote thousands of lines of verse.

One critic found her melodious, another superficial, and a third downright silly, quoting these lines from *The Deserter*:

> It is a sweet, albeit almost painful feeling
> To know we are regretted.

A friend who wrote an appreciation of her work after her early death said if her first verses had been honestly criticized instead of being overpraised L.E.L. might have written poems instead of lines.

Felicia Hemans was another writer of verses which appealed to the early Victorian woman, though it was not until her collected poems were published after her death, in 1835, that she became known. She was born in 1793, married a soldier from whom she eventually separated, and settled with her family of sons in Wales, supporting them by her writings. She wrote narrative poems, and many lyrics of a devotional nature, some of which were later turned into hymns.

Elizabeth Barrett Browning was acknowledged by all to be one of the major poets of her generation. Her quality was recognized from her earliest published works, though she was sometimes criticized for unevenness of style and occasional banal lines. In 1844 the volume of *Poems* which she brought out contained the moving "Cry of the Children," a deeply felt protest against the employment of children in factories. But she was not essentially a reformer; it was the exquisite *Sonnets from the Portuguese*, the expression of her love for Robert Browning, which established her fame when it was published in 1850.

All Mrs Browning's works were received with the respect due to the position she had attained, but praise was again tempered by criticism when *Aurora Leigh* was published in 1857. This was her most ambitious work: a romance in verse which ran to thousands of lines. It was an attempt to paint a picture of the England of her day, with its problems and difficulties, its family life, its tremendous social contrasts. Some critics complained of its length, others of the lack of significance in many of its passages; but all recognized the genius that lay behind the conception of such a work.

The novel-with-a-purpose, which was such a powerful force in the first half of the nineteenth century, began with Harriet Martineau. With her honesty, fine intellect, and humanitarian outlook, she was one of the most influential writers of the time. She lived from 1802 until 1876, and her writing life spanned more than fifty years.

A member of a Unitarian family, Harriet Martineau became interested in theology when she was still a girl, and her first writings were on religious subjects. But the conditions in which the labouring classes lived turned her mind to social science, and she began to write a series of tales embodying the principles and laws of political economy. She chose the story form because she wanted to interest the common people, to make them understand the nature of the political and economic forces which ruled their lives. Of one of these early stories, *The Rioters*, her friend Maria Weston Chapman wrote:

"It came home to the business and bosoms of the lace-makers of Derby and Nottingham with so much power that they instantly put themselves in communication with Miss Martineau, requesting a second story on Wages. . . . These tales are the first examples of a new application of the modern novel. To the biographical and philosophical novel, the descriptive and the historical novel, the romantic and the domestic novel, the fashionable and the religious novel, was now to be added the humanitarian or novel of reform."

Harriet Martineau was by instinct an educator, not an imaginative writer. She said herself, in her *Autobiography*, that she was incapable of constructing a plot, and had to base her stories on actual life, "amalgamating doctrine and narrative as far as possible." The results were not as heavy as might be imagined from that description; her stories were close-knit and logically worked out, but they also had a readable quality which was to make her name a household word within a few years. *Deerbrook*, published in 1839, was one of her two full-length novels, and was about a village doctor who lost his practice through holding unorthodox opinions. The other, *The Hour and the Man*, which came out in 1840, had for its hero Toussaint l'Ouverture, the Negro ex-slave, soldier, and liberator, and it was welcomed by the Abolitionists. Miss Martineau had travelled in America, and was a strong supporter of the anti-slavery movement.

She was an instinctive controversialist. Her early religious faith had changed to agnosticism, and she wrote fearlessly on that inflammable subject, provoking arguments which were published in pamphlets and in the Press. Mesmerism was another subject which brought her many opponents, but Miss Martineau wrote with the incisiveness of opinions sincerely held, and she could generally hold her own. Many of the leading writers admired her; Charlotte Brontë sought her out after reading *Deerbrook*, and the Carlyles were often her hosts. Her name appears frequently in the letters and memoirs of the period: Miss Martineau's advanced views, Miss Martineau's industry, Miss Martineau's wicked, *wicked* opinions—this last referring to an article defending the rationalist standpoint.

Harriet Martineau's gift to literature was for her own generation, as a later critic wrote. Her works were outdated before the end of the century, and only the legend of her personality remained. She left one phrase, however, which —with Ruskin's help, for he quoted it—has survived to become part of the common stock of home truths. In an early story, *Brooke and Brooke Farm*, she wrote: "The whole nation, the whole world, is obliged to him who makes corn grow where it never grew before; and yet more to him who makes two ears ripen where only one ripened before."

Elizabeth Cleghorn Gaskell was another writer of the humanitarian school, but, unlike Harriet Martineau, she was essentially a novelist, not a polemical writer. Like her celebrated contemporary, however, she took her settings and characters from life; her books were social documents as well as absorbingly interesting stories.

The wife of a Unitarian minister in Manchester, Mrs Gaskell had no need to travel far for her material; it was all around her, drably visible as she helped her husband with his work among the mill-hands in the back-streets. Her first books were about that world of hard labour and bitter want. She was not didactic; she did not offer any ready-made solutions, but was concerned only to show the life about her as it was lived. Her books were studies of character, closely observed and presented with sympathy and insight.

Mrs Gaskell's first book, *Mary Barton*, published in 1848, showed the appalling insecurity of the lives of mill-hands, dependent on the whims of their masters and the state of trade. The masters thought quite literally of their work-people as 'hands'; in the Lancashire mills many of them had no direct contact at all with their employees, who were hired by foremen spinners. From 1839 to 1841 there had been bad harvests, resulting in a fall in wages and a rise in prices; and in *Mary Barton* this was realistically described:

"For three years past trade had been getting worse and worse, and the price of provisions higher and higher. This disparity between the amount of the earnings of the working-classes and the price of their food occasioned, in more cases than could well be imagined, disease and death. They only wanted a Dante to record their sufferings."

The book roused public opinion and was discussed everywhere. Elizabeth Barrett Browning wrote of it to Miss Mitford: "There is power and truth—she can shake and she can pierce, but . . . I want more beauty, more air from the universal world; these class-books must always be defective as works of art." The reading public evidently did not consider it a class-book, for it sold in large numbers, and the reviews were full of high praise. A few critics thought the plot melodramatic, but the strength of the book lay in its truth and humanity, and this was fully recognized.

North and South, published in 1855, set out to show

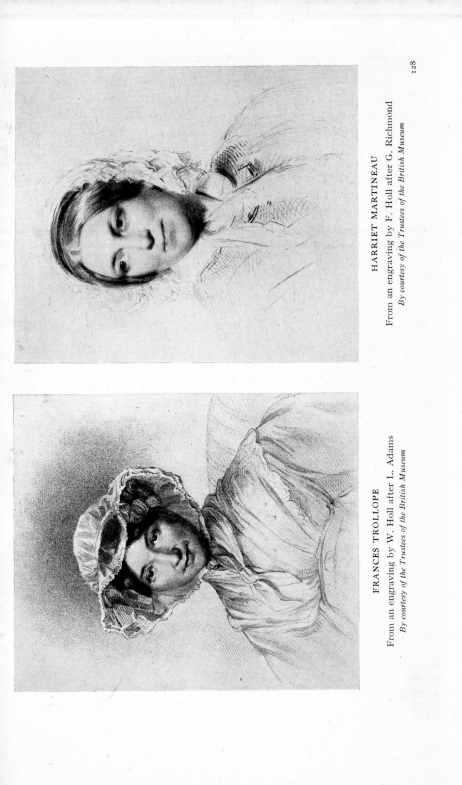

FRANCES TROLLOPE
From an engraving by W. Holl after L. Adams
By courtesy of the Trustees of the British Museum

HARRIET MARTINEAU
From an engraving by F. Holl after G. Richmond
By courtesy of the Trustees of the British Museum

128

BESIDE THE SEA

From a lithograph by J. Brandard for the song *Les Jolies filles d'Angleterre*

By courtesy of the Director of the Victoria and Albert Museum

another point of view: that the master of a mill could have principles and ideas, and be fair to his men. *Ruth*, which had come out earlier, was also a novel-with-a-purpose, for it set out to tell the story of a young semptress who had transgressed the moral law, and it was full of compassion for the weak and erring.

Mrs Gaskell had already endeared herself to a large public with *Cranford*, which came out in the same year as *Ruth*. This was something quite different from her other books; it was a study of life in a small country town. She had spent part of her youth in the little town of Knutsford, in Cheshire, and *Cranford* caught the rhythm of that quiet backwater. It was compared with Miss Mitford's *Our Village*, which had delighted readers twenty years before, but not to its disadvantage, and *Cranford* was a favourite among Mrs Gaskell's books from the time of its publication.

George Eliot (Mary Ann Evans), contemporary with Mrs Gaskell, is outside the scope of this brief survey, as she did not reach the height of her powers until the sixties; the early Victorian woman only knew of her, if at all, through the *Scenes of Clerical Life*, which ran as a serial in *Blackwood's Magazine* in 1857. She was already talked of in the literary world as the translator of a work from the German, *Leben Jesu*, and as the assistant editor, from 1851, of the *Westminster Review*.

The woman writer who made the strongest impact on her contemporaries was Charlotte Brontë. She was born in 1816, three years before George Eliot, and she was destined to die long before her great fellow-writer. It took George Eliot many years to establish her reputation, but Charlotte Brontë shook her readers into attention with her first book. "I always through my whole life liked to penetrate to the real truth," she wrote to a friend. "I like seeing the goddess in her temple, and handling the veil, and daring the dread glance."

Here indeed was a writer to startle the early Victorians. They could accept truth well enough when it was set down objectively by a Harriet Martineau, or with charity by an

I

Elizabeth Gaskell, and when it was concerned with social abuses which they could see for themselves when pointed out to them. But in *Jane Eyre* there was the kind of truth which had hitherto been kept well hidden by respectable authors: truth which brought to the surface women's frustrations, rebellions, passions. It was something new and alarming. And when the news came out that "Currer Bell," the author of *Jane Eyre*, was in fact a female, interest was reinforced by shock. It was incredible that any woman could indulge in such self-revelation, could write so plainly of what lay beneath the surface.

By the time Charlotte Brontë had published *Shirley*, in 1849, two years after the appearance of *Jane Eyre*, the curiosity and shock had disappeared, and she had taken her place in the first rank of writers. A review of *Shirley* in a woman's magazine typified the now general attitude to this new writer:

"Our novel literature has undergone a remarkable change of late years. Since the reign of Sir Walter Scott we have ceased to be satisfied with the picturesque and the historical, but long for something that takes a firm hold of our feelings, and stirs up our soul to its depths. . . . The cry now is— let it be something the mind can rest on as a truth, something founded on facts. *Jane Eyre* is intensely real. It may seem hard and ungenial, but in its main points it is sternly true to nature . . . it breaks new ground, is fresh and vigorous, its language is full of pith and nerve, and the interest it excites is strong and concentrated, the passion rising at times to a height of tragic intensity.

"In *Shirley*, the author's new book, we have the same strong characters, the same country-folk. The scene is laid in a manufacturing village of the West Riding; we have here woollen factories, and starved operatives thrown out of work by the new inventions. . . .

"The author is very bitter against *men* . . . she speaks as one outraged and aggrieved by their contemptuous treatment of her sex. We discern symptoms of a bitterness— we had almost said a fierceness—for which there is probably some good cause. But there are few women of strong

powers of mind, such as the author of this book unques-
tioningly is, who do not feel that the social position of
women is not at all what it should be, and hence she speaks
in her angry and indignant tone. . . .

"There is a want of a quiet, loving power, while of dis-
contented, rebellious power there is rather too much. When
the author has expended the latter force we may expect to
have some manifestations of her more serene and hopeful
spirit, and we trust that she will recognize in life a scene of
duty and conflict in which all must bear their part lovingly,
firmly, and, if possible, cheerfully."

If *Jane Eyre* shook the early Victorian reader *Wuthering
Heights*, Emily Brontë's masterpiece, had the force of a hurri-
cane. One reviewer said that she hardly knew of a more
gnarled, painful story; another called it a tale set against
granite. In 1847 *La Belle Assemblée* had a notice under the
heading of Literature:

"There has come out a new edition of *Wuthering Heights*
and *Agnes Grey*, with its new powerful and pathetic preface,
prefixed to the prose by the one survivor of the sister
authors, who, as Currer, Ellis, and Acton Bell, made such a
stir in the coteries a couple of winters ago. That three ladies,
living retired lives in a moorland Yorkshire parsonage,
should have broken into utterances so fiery, vigorous, and
uncouth in their vigour, as the novels in question, seemed
like a faery tale to those who have but lightly considered
what a mysterious thing is Genius, and who have not sufficiently remembered how it sometimes receives aliment and
impulse from the very circumstances which would seem the
most calculated to narrow and bind it."

It might appear to later eyes that the early Victorian
woman herself often received aliment and impulse from the
very circumstances which seemed the most calculated to
narrow and bind her; and the women writers of the day
added to her growing sense of strength and independence.
Genius and lesser author touched hands here; in the field of
literature, at least, they were accepted as individuals as well
as women. But not without protest. Here is a last word
from an early Victorian who wrote in the *Leader* in 1850:

"It is a melancholy fact, and against all political economy, that the group of female authors is becoming every year more multitudinous and more successful. . . . Wherever we carry our successful pens we find the place preoccupied by a woman. How many of us can write novels like Currer Bell, Mrs Gaskell, and fifty others, with their shrewd and delicate observations of life? What chance have we against Miss Martineau, so potent in many directions? Women have made an invasion of our legitimate domain; they write dramas, they write treatises. This is the march of mind, but where, oh where, are the dumplings? Does it never strike these delightful creatures that their little fingers were meant to be kissed, not to be inked? Women's proper sphere of activity is elsewhere. Are there not husbands, brothers, friends, lovers to coddle and console? Are there no stockings to darn, no purses to make, no braces to embroider? *My* idea of a perfect woman is one who can write, but won't."

EDUCATION

A N early-nineteenth-century reviewer once remarked
that women writers must possess more than ordinary
talent, since they could produce such excellent work
without having benefited from a classical education. What
astonishes the modern reader is that they should have been
able to write so well with hardly any education behind them
at all, let alone a classical education. They were fortunate in
that they had natural talent; the unfortunate women were
those who were not especially gifted, but who knew that
they needed formal education in order to become properly
developed human beings.

There was a still more urgent need for women's education; the whole question was bound up with the problem
of their freedom to work for a living. The high rate of emigration among young men at that period of commercial
expansion meant that there was a surplus of unmarried
middle-class women left at home. Many of these, on the
death of father or brother, had no means of support, and as
their education had been of the most superficial kind, they
rarely had any qualifications for earning a living. The
demand for better education came more insistently, however, from the sheltered girl, the daughter in the drawing-
room, tired of wasting an active mind on trivial amusements

and the pursuit of accomplishments. It was she, too, who had a growing conviction that a good education was the only basis on which she might be allowed political rights.

Mary Wollstonecraft had put something concrete into women's hands as far back as 1792, in her book *A Vindication of the Rights of Woman*. The book had been forged out of her own experience. After an unhappy early life, in which she had had to depend on her own resources, she managed to educate herself sufficiently to be able to support her younger brothers and sisters. She was in turn governess and publisher's reader, and felt most passionately the inferior status of women who had no men to support them. In her book she asked for equal education with men, equal opportunities to enter the professions, the right of married women to own property and to have a share in the custody of the children in case of a separation. She also wanted divorce to be made less difficult for women, and for men to be legally responsible for their illegitimate children.

It seems a reasonable enough list to us—especially as we, in our generation, enjoy all these rights and take them for granted. But the publication of the book, together with known facts of her unorthodox private life, marked Mary Wollstonecraft as dangerous and dissolute. Her ideas were bitterly attacked, by women as well as by men. Right up to mid-Victorian times her name was blackguarded and her private character made a peg for moral sermons. But she nevertheless woke a germ of revolt in the most respectable heads, and there were few of the Victorian pioneers in education who had not read her pamphlet.

In 1843 Mrs Hugo Reid published *A Plea For Woman*, a book which had a large sale. It was a rational, balanced series of arguments for the improved status of woman as an individual, and the chapter on education brought out a good many points which had been ignored in the numerous attacks which were then being made on women's attempts to obtain a better education. It was one of these attacks, in the *Edinburgh Review* for April-July 1841, which decided Mrs Reid to write a counter-attack. She pointed out that in almost every town of a few thousand inhabitants, there were endowed schools for the benefit of the sons of citizens, but none for the daughters, who were entirely neglected. She went on to ask: "If woman be naturally more feeble of intellect than man, surely she has, on that very account, the greater need of all the advantages which education can bestow?"

The attacks went on. Mrs Reid's counterblast was itself assailed in turn; not with equally reasonable arguments, but with scoffing and abuse. A newspaper asked: "Of what use is education to the weaker sex? The professions and public offices are very properly not open to women. The most proper occupations for women are teaching young ladies, especially religion and drawing." Another declared: "Too many publications are being published, aimed at the intellectual improvement of the female sex."

The popular writer Mrs Abdy in *La Belle Assemblée* hastened to reassure her readers in the first paragraph of an article headed "Educated Women":

"Let not my readers be alarmed at the title of my paper. I am not going to advocate the claims of lady-colleges on the one hand, or cookery schools on the other. I hold that education to be best which not only fits a woman for the station which she is likely to fill in the world, but which so strengthens her character, that, should fortune see fit to elevate her to a higher, or depress her to a lower station, she would still be able to act in becoming accordance with her duties."

Mrs Abdy went on for some length, coming at last to the conclusion that womanly patience was the highest end of all female education.

The majority of parents agreed in principle with Mrs Abdy's sentiments, for they either had their daughters educated at home on the lines she laid down, or sent them away to boarding schools after the age of twelve. It was at these establishments that the feminine virtues, together with the more showy of feminine accomplishments, could have a high polish put on them for the marriage market.

Thackeray has given us the essence of these schools in Miss Pinkerton's Academy, and a comparison between his fiction and the factual accounts of schooldays found in memoirs and biographies show that he did not exaggerate. Every town had its boarding-schools; at the fashionable resorts there were dozens. Frances Power Cobbe, one of the most vigorous-minded of the Victorian writers, tells us in her *Life* that there were at least a hundred such establishments in Brighton in 1836, when she went to school there. The average fees were about £130 a year, but her own school-bills for two years amounted to £1000 because of the exorbitant extras. She gives such a clear and exact account of her life at this school that I cannot do better than quote from her autobiography:

"The education of women was probably at its lowest ebb [then]. It was at that period more pretentious than it had ever been before . . . and it was likewise more shallow and senseless than can easily be believed. . . . The din of our large double schoolrooms was something frightful. Sitting in either of them, four pianos might be heard going at once in rooms above and around us, while at numerous tables . . . there were girls reading aloud to the governesses and reciting lessons in English, French, German, and Italian. This hideous clatter continued the entire day till we went to bed at night . . . there being no time whatever allowed for recreation.

"On Saturday afternoons, instead of play, there was a terrible ordeal generally known as the Judgment Day. On the table were the books wherein our evil deeds of the week were recorded: *e.g.*, having our shoe-strings untied, or stooping, or being impertinent. . . . Anything more ridiculous than the scene which followed can hardly be conceived. I have seen no less than nine young ladies obliged to sit for hours, like naughty babies, with their faces to the wall; half of them quite of marriageable age, and all dressed, as was *de rigeur* with us every day, in full evening attire of silk or muslin, with gloves and kid slippers. . . .

"All the pupils were daughters of men of standing . . . but all this fine human material was deplorably wasted. Nobody dreamed that any one of us could in later life be more or less than an 'Ornament of Society.' That a pupil in that school should ever become an artist or authoress . . .

would have been looked upon as a deplorable dereliction. Not that which was good in itself or useful to the community or even that which would be delightful to ourselves, but that which would make us admired in society, was the *raison d'être* of each requirement. Everything was taught us in the inverse ratio of its true importance. At the bottom of the scale were Morals and Religion, and at the top were Music and Dancing: miserably poor music too. . . . Our English studies embraced one long, awful lesson each week to be repeated to the schoolmistress by a class, in history one week, in geography the week following. Our first class, I remember, had once to commit to memory—Heaven alone knows how—no less than thirteen pages of Wood-houselee's *Universal History*! . . . It is almost needless to add that the heterogeneous studies pursued in this helter-skelter fashion were of the smallest possible utility in later life; all real education worthy of the name had to be begun on our return home, after we had been pronounced 'finished.' "

That was at an expensive, fashionable school. One can imagine what was provided by the cheap imitators of young ladies' academies. The newspapers of the period are full of advertisements of these schools, all stressing refinement, or 'tone,' or elegance, or moral instruction, or a combination of any or all of them.

Even more numerous are advertisements for governesses in private families. If one had a family of daughters it was more economical to employ a governess than to send three or four girls to boarding-school. Many families shared a governess and visiting masters with neighbours or relations, so cutting the cost down farther still. The picture of the Victorian governess has come down to us deeply stamped with the features of Jane Eyre: a woman of intelligence, sensibility, and deep feelings, condemned by poverty to a life of repressions and frustrations. This was a true enough picture in many cases—but it was equally true that numbers of women of inferior intellect applied for positions as governesses when they might have been better advised to look lower on the social scale and take domestic posts. A letter to the editor of *La Belle Assemblée* puts this point of

view, an unusual one compared with the general correspondence on the subject which went on at intervals throughout the first half of the century:

"MY DEAR MADAM,

"I have for several months observed the manner in which
you have been endeavouring to place English governesses
in a better position in society; your object is most kind and
praiseworthy. I can speak feelingly, for though, during my
many months' residence in the abode of strangers, I have met
with very much kind consideration, and as far as the English
natural temperament will permit, even sympathy; yet the
constant sense that a governess is deemed inferior in position . . . is sometimes more than a sensitive mind can endure.

"But at the same time, my dear Madam, is there not much
to be said on the other side? I must remind you that many
governesses of the present day are not ladies. . . . In their
own homes they meet with no more refinement in mind and
manners than in the servants' hall of their employers, and
these often expect more indulgence than any real lady looks
for. I allow that the position of governess requires amendment; but at the same time a good cause may be injured by
going too far. Trusting your endeavours to promote
amelioration where much needed will be both judicious and
successful,

"I am, dear Madam,
"Yours in Sincerity,
"A GOVERNESS"

The writer of this letter was typical of the majority of
those who became governesses: a member of the middle
classes who was forced to earn her living in the only respectable manner open to her. Conscious of her lack of real
qualifications for teaching, she was sensitive to the change
in her social condition, yet was appreciative of "kind consideration" and thankful, no doubt, to have a roof over her
head and enough to eat.

This state of affairs led to the worst kind of exploitation
by employers. *Punch* in 1845 had a slashing attack on this
advertisement in the *Evangelical Magazine*:

"WANTED: a Young Person, of decided piety, about 22 years of age, to take charge and educate three children under twelve years. She must be capable of imparting a sound English education, with French and music. Anyone who would feel anxious for the welfare of the children will be treated as one of the family, and may realize the comforts of a home. Salary, £8 per annum. Apply direct to G. I., Cheapside."

"What a Christian!" jibed *Punch*. "G. I., with his fondness for decided piety, has interested us. We are anxious that, for his magnificent £8 per annum—by the way, what may he give the boy who cleans the knives and forks?—he should have the very best instruction for his babes purchasable for such a liberal sum."

A letter in *The Times*, a few years later, brought forward an even shabbier case:

"SIR,

"As the following circumstances may serve to expose the abominable meanness of some persons who require the services of the above valuable class of society, I hope you will give it a place in your widely circulated journal. In reply to an advertisement in the *Times*, a daily governess of highly respectable connexions called on a lady, living in a splendidly furnished house, not a hundred yards from Notting Hill Square, who, it seemed, had four children . . . requiring tuition in music, French, German, drawing, and the usual routine of a polite education. After stating that four hours a day would be requisite, the governess naturally expected a handome renumeration, but, Sir, you may well conceive her astonishment at the liberal offer of eight shillings per week—one penny per hour for each pupil! I really was so disgusted with the circumstance that I determined to expose it. But, Sir, I believe it is a common case.

"I am, Sir,
"Yours etc.,
"A CONSTANT READER"

It was to help women subject to this kind of treatment that the Governesses' Benevolent Institution came into being in the early forties. A clergyman, the Rev. David Laing, was its energetic honorary secretary. An employment registry for governesses was added to the Institution, but Laing and his friends soon realized that these women could not command adequate salaries unless they were properly educated for their work. It was decided to give lectures, not only to dwellers in the Institution, but also to other governesses who came there for registration.

The scheme was strongly supported by Frederick Denison Maurice, Professor of Divinity at King's College, London, and other members of the faculty there. They formed themselves into a Committee of Education, and taught and examined at the Institution without fees. About the same time the Hon. Amelia Murray, a Maid of Honour to the Queen, was collecting funds for the establishment of a college for women. Miss Murray suggested to the Committee that the two schemes might be combined. She was able to interest her royal mistress in the proposed college, and in the Report of the Institution for 1847 one reads that "the Queen has permitted the use of the Royal name; that a connexion has been formed with a body of gentlemen, not only eminent for their professional abilities, but all of them experienced in some form of instruction; that a house had been purchased adjacent to the Home . . . and arrangements had been made to secure the supervision of ladies of rank and talent; and that the committee had begun in 1847 to examine governesses, and to grant them certificates according to their merits."

In March 1848 Queen's College in Harley Street was opened with an inaugural lecture by F. D. Maurice, who explained its aims. Maurice was an outstanding figure in a group of remarkable men, among them Charles Kingsley and Alfred Tennyson, whose vision of an ideal women's college in his poem *The Princess* had not long been published.

The curriculum of Queen's College might well have been startling to those brought up on accomplishments and fashionable boarding-schools. Maurice himself taught theology, Kingsley took English literature, and Sterndale Bennett taught music. The other subjects included ancient and modern languages, natural philosophy, mathematics, dancing, and the fine arts. The "ladies of rank and talent" were called Lady Visitors; they were nominally chaperons, women of prestige who attended the lectures in rotation and were responsible for discipline.

From the beginning Frederick Maurice laid down standards, the most notable being the principle of non-competition and the absence of rewards and punishments. His ideas on girls' education were far ahead of his time, and it was the greatest good fortune that he should have been the man to help found the first real school for women, which, in turn, was to produce some of the outstanding educators of the century.

In 1852 the College separated from the Institution. The classes were now open to all; besides the day school, lectures were held in the evening. The celebrated pair, Miss Beale and Miss Buss, both attended lectures at Queen's in their early years. Dorothea Beale relates how delighted she and her sisters were to find that it was possible for women to pass examinations at Queen's. She returned to the College as Tutor in 1849, leaving seven years later to teach for a time in a provincial school, and then to become principal of Cheltenham Ladies' College. Miss Buss ran her own private school in North London, the school which was later to become famous as the North London Collegiate School, the pattern for the system of high schools established later in the century.

The year 1849 was important in the history of women's education, for in that year was established the "Ladies' College in Bedford Square," destined as Bedford College to become the first college for women in the University of London. It was founded through the efforts of Elizabeth Reid, the widow of a doctor, but no connexion, so far as it is known, of the redoubtable Mrs Hugo Reid of a decade earlier. Elizabeth Reid was one of a group of social reformers; she was a close friend of Harriet Martineau, and assisted that energetic woman to "improve local housing conditions and to give tenants an opportunity of acquiring their own houses in time." She supported the anti-slavery movement and everything else of a philanthropic character that was brought to her notice.

Mrs Reid had from her girlhood dreamed of a college for women, a place of "combined lectures, examinations, and exercises," where ladies could have a liberal education at a moderate expense. It was not until she was nearly sixty that she was able to do anything practical about her early ambition; her first serious attempts to collect support for the proposed college did not begin until the eighteen-forties.

It was unlikely that Mrs Reid knew of the early plans going forward for Queen's College. She was a Unitarian, and Queen's was closely connected with those who belonged to the Established Church. When Queen's College opened, however, Mrs Reid was interested and sympathetic; she did not consider it a rival. She wanted to establish, not a school, but a college for women that would approximate to university level. By 1849 there was enough interest in Mrs Reid's scheme to justify a start being made at her house. Professors were engaged to lecture, and Mrs Reid invited ladies of her acquaintance to attend. The scheme expanded. Mrs Reid undertook to back the college financially for two years, and a house was rented in Bedford Square. More professors were engaged; a prospectus was drawn up; various ladies' committees came into being; a body of Lady Visitors was formed.

The Lady Visitors, as at Queen's College, were necessary as chaperons. They were expected "to endeavour to uphold decorum and Silence in the Institution, and enforce in the Class Room attendance and punctuality . . . and to direct their attention to the ventilation and general comfort of the room." It was also hoped that the young ladies would look to the Lady Visitors as friends to whom they could go for advice and assistance.

The college was not the immediate success hoped for by Mrs Reid. The ideal was, in the founder's mind, an educational establishment of university rank, but there was no early prospect of that ideal being fulfilled. The first prospectus stated that "ladies were admitted over the age of twelve years," so it had to begin as a school. The most serious cause of its lack of support, however, was its Nonconformist connexion in a society which belonged chiefly to the Established Church.

The first years of the college's existence were difficult, mostly on account of financial troubles; and they were also scarred by internal dissensions between the council of the college and some of the professors on matters of religion. Sectarian beliefs and prejudices were deeply rooted, and during the first three years there were many resignations. At one point it seemed as if the college would not be able to continue its work, but it struggled on and survived.

The continuation of its development lies far outside the scope of this book. Its present position as the senior women's college in London University sufficiently indicates the success which came after the long years of effort.

What of that other early Victorian woman—the labourer's daughter, the factory-hand? What education did she receive? She had no governess, no mother with time to drill her in Mangnall's *Questions* and the use of the globes. The bulk of working-class women could neither read nor write. The *Return of Marriage Registers* for 1851 shows that in that year, out of 154,000 women married in England nearly 70,000 signed their names with marks. In the same year Samuel Smiles wrote:

"The annual publication of the Minutes of the Committee of Council on Education reminds us from time to time of the extremely defective provision made for the education of the people of this country. The Exhibition in Hyde Park may show that Britain can make more perfect machines than any European nation; the Agricultural Society's Show at Windsor may exhibit our superiority in the breeding and rearing of stock; but these Minutes of Council show that while we make perfect machines and breed first-rate cattle, the rearing, training, and education of our men and women, especially the lower strata of the labouring classes, is about the worst in Europe."

There had been charity schools in the eighteenth century; religious instruction, needlework, and resignation seem to have been the chief subjects for girls. Towards the end of that century the Sunday School movement began to exercise a great influence; children were taught their letters in order to be able to read the Bible, which was often used as a primer. Two women were mainly responsible for the rapid growth of these schools: Sarah Trimmer and Hannah More. Mrs Trimmer, a writer of moral tales for the young, opened a school at Brentford in 1786, and added handwork and other useful occupations to her Sunday School teaching, using the school during the week for that purpose. Her ideas became known far outside her own district, and were copied in many places. Hannah More, with her sister Martha, opened a Sunday School in Somerset in 1789, and within a few years they were supervising the secular as well as the religious instruction of about three thousand children and parents.

Sarah Trimmer and Hannah More set a pattern which was followed by religious and philanthropic persons right up to the eighteen-thirties and -forties, and, indeed, up to the time when state education became established late in the century. These small schools served some purpose, but none of them provided any real education, and most of them degenerated into dame-schools, where the children were crowded into small rooms and made to repeat moral maxims and pages of the Bible parrot-fashion. The fees were a few pence a week; the dame keeping the school made a very meagre living, unless she was subsidized by the local great house.

In the large industrial towns the more progressive-minded factory-owners attempted to provide rudimentary schooling for the girls and boys employed in their mills, though these young people were often too exhausted at the end of a long day's labour to benefit by any teaching. Robert Owen, one of the most enlightened employers of the early nineteenth century, provided schools for the children of his workpeople at his mills in New Lanark. There was an infants' school where children between the ages of three and

A PRIZE BABY SHOW

"You have nursed a Charming Child, and I have much pleasure in awarding you this interesting volume on Plain Domestic Cookery! I also 'honourably mention' the dear Baby's Papa!"

J. Leech

From the author's collection

THE PARLIAMENTARY FEMALE

FATHER OF THE FAMILY: Come, dear, we seldom go out together now. Can't you take us all to the play to-night?

MISTRESS OF THE HOUSE AND M.P.: How you talk, Charles! Don't you see that I am too busy? I have a Committee to-morrow morning, and I have my speech on the Great Crochet Question to prepare for the evening.

J. Leech (from *Punch's Almanack*)

six were encouraged to observe and learn by means of play-things, and a school for those between six and twelve, where reading, writing, and arithmetic were taught, together with needlework for girls. In the evening these schools were used for what we would now call adult education: the work-people themselves, women as well as men, could come for instruction in reading and writing.

There had been a movement for adult education for some years, mainly fostered by the mechanics' institutes and young men's mutual improvement societies which flourished in many towns. Following on these came the Industrial Schools for Young Women, where "the instruction given is intellectual as well as domestic. Reading, writing, and general information are alternated with knitting, sewing, instruction in cookery, domestic management, and the ways of making a house comfortable."

Together with these unco-ordinated experiments in edu-cating the labouring classes there was a growing movement to establish some system of elementary education on a national scale. Two large religious organizations had already founded schools: the National Society, which taught the principles of the Established Church, and the British and Foreign School Society, which was a Noncon-formist body. These organizations were voluntarily sup-ported, but they also received Treasury grants, as did a few others which opened Unitarian or secular schools. In 1839 a Committee of Council on Education was set up by the Government; this was the forerunner of the Board of Edu-cation, which developed from it at the end of the century. The Committee of Council was responsible for "the Appli-cation of any sums voted by Parliament for the purpose of promoting public education." It did not attempt to control policy, but made yearly grants to the existing organizations for the purpose of extending the educational work already being done, tacitly agreeing to the religious bias of all such teaching.

The strong religious differences of the time were reflected in the tug-of-war rivalry between the Church schools and those run by Nonconformists or secularists. Undenomina-

K

tional teaching did not come in until the last quarter of the century.

In the town schools large numbers of boys and girls were taught under the 'mutual' system, a method which enabled one or two monitors—scholars who were one lesson ahead of the children they taught—to instruct the others. There were no separate classrooms; the schools were contained within one large hall, in which groups of boys and girls of varying ages recited the lesson after their monitor-instructor.

This system had been tried in Madras by Andrew Bell, a schoolmaster who had taken Holy Orders and gone out to India. Finding it difficult to obtain properly qualified masters there, he has worked out a method by which the scholars themselves did the teaching. He wrote a pamphlet called, "An Experiment in Education," which came to the notice of a Quaker educator in England, Joseph Lancaster, who had had similar ideas. When the British and Foreign School Society was formed, in 1808, Lancaster's monitorial system was adopted for its schools. In 1811 the Church of England founded the National Society for the Education of the Poor, and appointed, as its first Superintendent, Andrew Bell, who had returned from India. Thus the rivals followed the same pattern of education, though they differed on the principles of religious instruction.

The monitorial system had many defects, but, at least, it gave a chance of learning to read and write to thousands of children who would otherwise have remained illiterate. At a time when few men or women could be induced to take up teaching, owing to the wretched pay, the monitor-instructor served a useful purpose.

In the country districts few children had the chance of going to school at all, except to the dame-schools which might exist in cottages. Even when better schools did exist, greedy or desperate parents sent their children at an early age to work in the fields in order to earn a few shillings, rather than let them "waste time larnin' to cipher and know about things as don't concern 'em," as one mother said to an Inspector of a Parochial School Union. It was probably this attitude that was responsible for the answers made to another Inspector—in 1851—when he tested a group of country children on the knowledge they had managed to pick up. One girl said the Gospels were written by Shadrach, Meshach, and Abed-nego. Another said that the Queen's name was Mary Magdalene. Asked what an island was, a child replied that it was "a small house by the waterside." Prophecy was defined as fortune-telling, and the number of Commandments was put at fifteen.

In spite of the philanthropists, the voluntary bodies, and the growing State support of schools, the general level of education in the labouring and artisan classes was very low in the forties and fifties. And it is this fact which underlies everything that appears in the next chapter, on women's work.

XIII

WOMEN'S WORK

*'Genteel' Employment—A New Invention—The Sweated Needle-trades—
Home Industries—The Mills—Low Wages and Standards of Living—
Attempts at Reform—The Ten Hours Bill—Women and Children in Coal-
mines—Legislation*

THE need to educate the governess led to the establishment of better schools for girls, and, eventually, to the
raising of the status of women teachers. There were
still large numbers of women, however, who wanted to
work, but did not want to teach. Why could not there be
female designers in industry? So demanded one lady in a
Northern newspaper. And Eliza Cook pressed home this
question in her *Journal*:

"We do not see why women should not be much more
extensively employed in the decorative arts generally; as, for
instance, in copper and steel-plate engraving, in wood
engraving, and in all sorts of illustrative art connected with
literature. Why should they not be as competent, by proper
training, to execute a pattern for a dress, a chandelier, or a
grate, as to choose one? There is a great deal of the clerical
work of the day which could be performed by women as
well as men."

Amateur artists there were in plenty among the middle
class, but there were also women who wanted genuine
instruction in craftsmanship, and to be able to sell their
wares. The first successful attempt to put 'art' on a professional footing was made by a Miss Wallace, in 1851. She
had invented a method of applying colours in a decorative
pattern on glass, and she had the good sense to patent her
invention. A contemporary number of the *Builder* said:

"All our ideas of Oriental splendour. . . are realized in the sober actualities of British Decorative Art in Glass by Wallace's Patent. The lustre of silver and gold, the fiery sparkle of the ruby, amethyst, and every actual or imaginable gem . . . may be combined at a moderate cost, and without a vestige of mere gaudy glitter, in the decorations of the mansions of the gentlemen of England."

A Ladies' Guild was set up for the purpose of teaching Miss Wallace's art, and the popular journals welcomed the project. *La Belle Assemblée* thought it would provide "eligible and remunerative employment for ladies, without requiring them to descend from their rank as gentlewomen," but Eliza Cook, in her *Journal*, took a more robustly feminist view:

"We take a warm interest in everything calculated to increase the self-dependence of the female sex through the exertion of their own industry. . . . They are educated into dependence; . . . marriage is the prize which woman is taught to regard as her 'main chance,' except in the case of a few stronger natures, who believe in . . . the possibility of realizing true happiness from the cultivation of their own powers and the exertion of their own industry."

The Guild had a constitution and rules. Ladies wishing to be instructed in the art of decorative glass design were to pay an admission fee of one pound, and then two shillings a week. After a period of six months they were elected as associates, and shared in the profits of the venture. They could not then be subjected to dismissal, but by the sentence of their compeers and through "well-proven misconduct."

The Ladies' Guild was a private venture which happened to have influential supporters in London, and so became financially successful. It did not solve the problem of the thousands of women who tried to find 'genteel' employment without any such backing, and who, in the end, had to sink into the sweated needle-trades. The daughters of unfortunate professional people and once-prosperous tradesmen who had suffered reverses were compelled to turn to the needle to support themselves if they had no capacity for anything else. The already crowded trades of the milliner, the dressmaker, and the mantua-maker became little better than slave-trades in the hands of unscrupulous employers.

There was never any lack of apprentices for bonnet-making or dressmaking; parents who knew factory labour were often determined to put their daughters to less coarsening work, and somehow found the premiums of £30 to £60 which were demanded for an apprenticeship. But there was little to choose in horror between young girls exploited in the factory and sweated in the workroom.

The Children's Employment Commission of 1843 brought to public notice the appalling conditions of labour in the sewing trades. Mr R. D. Grainger, a well-known anatomist of the time, was one of the commissioners, and he collected a great deal of evidence. He showed that apprentices worked for long hours in unventilated, comfortless workrooms, received no wages for two or three years, and were badly fed and lodged. One of the commentators on the Report said:

[The Report reveals] there are masses of human creatures, of tender age and sex, whose lives are prematurely shortened by an excess of labour. Women of the higher and middle classes, tender mothers and gentle daughters among them, [can now learn] the true secrets of the labour which clothed them in luxury and fineness; whilst legislators and men interested in the progress of public health and morality are, by the vital information thus obtained, led to some of the causes of the enormous annual waste of human life, through consumption, and of the deterioration, both physical and moral, which assists to throw so many youthful females on our streets."

It was stated that at the height of the London season, and especially during the week preceding a royal Drawing-room, work-girls often sewed for twenty hours, their meals being brought to them as they worked. A fashionable wedding or a mourning order, especially the latter, often meant all-night work for the sempstresses.

The publication of the Report roused a good deal of feeling and brought strong protests against the prevailing conditions from every kind of newspaper. There were articles in *Fraser's*, one of the most widely read journals; in the *Edinburgh Review*, another influential paper, and, of course, in the magazines mainly read by women. Criticism was forthright:

"It is the need for true education, it is a low mental condition, which leads the lady of fashion and wealth into issuing preposterous commands for orders at excessively short notice, for the simple reason that because she can afford to pay, her ignorance and frivolous will must be laws."

"Madame So-and-So protests she has her bonnets from Paris, her mantles from the Palais Royal. Her 'Paris' is some garret where four faded, patient girls stitch away at some 'Paris bonnets' at a few halfpence each . . . where pale wash, dignified with the name of tea, stale red herrings, and musty bread or cold potatoes are the only nourishment that enter there. This, then, is the Paris of our English milliners. Well may they afford to go clad in purple and fine linen, to amass fortunes, to revel in luxurious homes, in hypocritical servility in the carpeted floors of Regent Street —when every robe they wear is wrung from the lifeblood of beings of their own sex."

Besides the sempstresses employed in the workrooms of the dressmakers, there was a vast army of sewing-women who worked at home, making shirts and trousers. These were the 'slop-workers,' the worst-paid of all. They sewed from early morning till late at night, and even then were unable to earn more than three or four shillings a week. They were ruthlessly overworked by contractors who supplied the cheap shops; and there were always fresh workers to take the places of those who went blind or died prematurely, for it was to this type of plain sewing that the unskilled woman turned when she no longer had anyone to support her.

The evidence which Mr Grainger collected about slop-workers' lives was even more horrifying than the facts he had given about apprentices, and it received publicity on a national scale. Thomas Hood's poem *The Song of the Shirt* appeared in the Christmas number of *Punch* that year, and was quoted in books, in articles, on public platforms, in drawing-rooms, and in committee-rooms where men like Lord Ashley[1] and his friends were studying ways of combating these terrible social evils by legislation. In the following year John Bright quoted at length from the Children's Commission during a discussion on the Factory Bill; he pointed out that sewing-women were in as great need of protection as factory workers.

Reform came slowly. An association was formed, with Lord Ashley as president, which aimed at shortening the hours of apprentices, stopping Sunday work, improving conditions in workrooms, and securing amenities for girls without a home. Appeals were made to employers, some of whom joined the association, but they were in a minority; the abuses went on. In 1856 Mr Grainger found that very little change had been made by the employers as a whole.

The appeal was now to the ladies who were, in the last analysis, responsible for the rush-orders and consequent inhuman hours of work. A group of prominent Society women supported the appeal, but little was actually done on an organized scale during our period of 1837 to 1857; the major reforms were not to come until many decades later.

The amelioration of the slop-workers' lives began with the formation of a society which set out to bypass the contractor who distributed the work and who also took a large share of the payments. With this middleman eliminated, the sewing-women's earnings went up, and though the rate paid was still miserably low, it was felt that some reform had begun. The problem was too great, however, to be solved by one philanthropic association. This sweated industry was a disgrace to the Victorian Age until the end of the century, even after many attempts had been made to frame legislation which would protect its victims. The main fight for reform lies outside our period.

Mention should be made, though, of Caroline Chisholm's original and successful scheme for encouraging large numbers of sewing-women to emigrate to Australia, thus easing the crowded market at home, and supplying the new colony

[1] Anthony Ashley Cooper, who later became the seventh Earl of Shaftesbury.

with much-needed workers—and wives. I have sketched
the career of this astonishing early Victorian in another
chapter; I am concerned here with noting that Mrs Chisholm, who had lived and travelled in Australia, urged
unemployed sewing-women to emigrate, promoted schemes
whereby they were helped with their passage-money, and
arranged to have them assisted to suitable situations when
they reached Australia. She warned them that they would
have to turn their hands to all kinds of work; but she also
gave them hope of security and self-respect.

The conditions of women workers were as bad, and often
worse, in other trades than sewing. There were the framework knitters—the 'stockeners,' who made stockings.
This had been a prosperous cottage industry during the
preceding century, when men's fashions had called for elegant stockings, finely embroidered. The more sober styles
of the early nineteenth century lessened the demand. Knit-
ting-frames worked by steam were introduced in 1846;
these frames were rented out to home-workers, and the
finished stockings collected and paid for—with deductions
—by a middleman.

Glove-making was also a cottage industry, centred mainly
in Worcestershire. The women workers were highly skilled,
and were renowned for the excellence of their craftsmanship.
The fashion for French gloves which had begun after the
Napoleonic wars hit the trade badly, and by the forties there
was much distress in cottage homes which had traditionally
been dependent on gloving for a livelihood. A note in the
Worcester Chronicle in 1843 gives a glimpse into conditions
prevailing at that time:

"The Glove Trade: As an instance of the state of depression of this branch of manufacture we may state that a
manufacturer recently sold 470 dozens of gloves at sixpence
a dozen, the mere cutting of which, let alone all the numerous
other operations requisite to complete the gloves, did not
cost less than eightpence a dozen."

Then there was lace-making, which was both a home and
a factory industry. The dresses of the period were profusely

trimmed with lace, handmade when possible. This enabled thousands of women and girls to earn money at home; but low prices were given for their skilled work, and they had to bend over their lace-cushions for many hours a day before they could make a few shillings. Tambouring, the making of flowers on lace, was a similar home industry, and was equally badly paid.

Lace-making had been a factory industry since early in the century. The machines were kept going for twenty hours at a time, and needed constant attention. Men tended the machines, but women and children refilled the bobbins and did the winding and carding. A lace-runner worked at home, embroidering the designs on the foundation net. The factory distributed this part of the work through a 'lace-mistress,' who took her share of the meagre wage paid to the lace-runner.

It was not only in the traditional trades that women were employed; they helped in the heavier industries. Nail-making employed many thousands of female workers. In 1851 there were 10,000 in the service of 'nailers,' who gave out light rods to be hammered into nails. Some women were able to make a thousand nails a day, but the pay, as always, was wretchedly small.

Women were employed in pin-making, in screw-making, in the manufacture of steel pens, in button-making, in glass-polishing, in various processes of pottery manufacture, and in match-making—one of the most dangerous trades of all, as the phosphorus attacked the workers and caused disease. The machinery in factories was unfenced, and during the entire period covered by this outline there are terrible accounts in the newspapers—especially in the Northern papers—of machinery catching women's hair and scalping them.

It is probable that the largest number of women were employed in the textile-mills: in the cotton-, woollen-, flax-, and silk-mills which had begun to cover the Midlands and the northern part of England. For centuries women had helped in the making of cloth; it had been the chief cottage industry, and the weaver with a loom in the main room of

his home had always relied on wife and children to assist
him.

The Industrial Revolution in the early days of the nineteenth century, which brought machinery for cloth-making
into use on an enormous scale, killed this old cottage craft.
And as the economy of working-class life had been built on
family industry of this kind, and as men's wages in the mills
were so low, many wives had to go into the mills too—to be
paid on an even lower scale.

Women worked a fourteen-to-sixteen-hour day for less
than ten shillings a week; sometimes they worked part of
the night to earn an extra shilling or two. The work
and conditions were brutalizing, and the social effects were
deeply, and often bitterly, felt. Women went back to the
mills within a fortnight of the birth of a baby, who had to be
left in the care of other small children at home, or with an
old woman past any other kind of work. There was no time
for cooking at home; the family lived on tea and bread, oat-
meal porridge, and a large dish of potatoes for dinner, with
occasionally some bacon added to it. No proper housework
was done; there was little comfort. In Mrs Gaskell's novel
Mary Barton, the principal characters of which are mill-
workers, one of them says (Chapter 10):

"'It's Prince Albert as ought to be asked how he'd like
his missus to be from home when he comes in, tired and
worn, and wanting some one to cheery him; and, maybe,
her to come in by and by, just as tired and down in th'
mouth; and how he'd like for her never to be at home to see
to th' cleaning of his house, or to keep a bright fire in the
grate, let alone his meals being all hugger-mugger. . . . I'd
be bound, prince as he is, if his missus served him so, he'd
go off to a gin-palace, or summat o' that kind. So why can't
he make a law agin poor folks' wives working in factories?'"

The answer was not simple. While it was true that some
married women worked for money to buy finery, it is clear
from the many Government investigations on wages that
the majority of women who worked in the textile factories
did so from necessity.

Hours were eventually shortened. Lord Ashley had been

trying for years to bring in a shorter working-day for factories—for men as well as for women. After repeated setbacks, he saw a Bill through Parliament in 1844 which limited the hours of work to twelve a day, though only for women and young persons; it also provided for the fencing of machinery in factories. In 1847 another Bill, popularly called the Ten Hours Bill, reduced the hours still further, to fifty-eight hours a week. A further Act in 1850 established a 'normal' working-day for women and children over thirteen, and gave them a half-day on Saturday.

These reduced hours enabled women to have some leisure on which they could depend, and there was soon evidence that the standard of housekeeping began to go up as a consequence. They even found time to attend evening classes. "The New School for Wives," the subject of an article in *Household Words* in 1852, comments on the gratifying number of factory women who regularly attended classes after the day's work was done.

The blackest stain on the early Victorian era was not the factory conditions—bad as they were—but the employment of women and children in the coal-mines. They worked underground as 'hurriers,' loading wagons with coal, and as 'drawers,' pulling the wagons along places which were too low for the pit-ponies. They also carried loads of coal on their backs. As a 'drawer,' a woman had a belt round her waist and a chain passing between her legs; she moved on hands and feet, holding on to a rope. The roads underground were steep, and she dragged the wagon of coal by the chain, holding the rope. For this labour she was paid about two shillings for a twelve-to-sixteen-hour day.

Disraeli drew a dramatic picture of these women in his novel *Sybil*:

"Oaths that men might shudder at issued from lips born to breathe words of sweetness. Yet these are to be, some are, the mothers of England! . . . Naked to the waist . . . clad in canvas trousers. . . an English girl hauls and hurries tubs of coal up subterranean roads, dark, precipitous, and plashy; circumstances that seem to have escaped the notice of the Society for the Abolition of Negro Slavery. Those

worthy gentlemen, too, appear to have been singularly unconscious of the suffering of the little trappers, which was
remarkable, as many of them were in their own employ."

The little trappers were the boys and girls who also
worked far underground, closing the traps after the women.

In June 1842 Lord Ashley made a speech in Parliament
in which he gave in detail evidence of the terrible conditions
of women's work in the mines. He spoke of the danger of
accidents from fire-damp and other causes, of the water in
the pits, of the complete exhaustion which followed a day's
labour. Above all, he stressed the demoralization which
was the inevitable result of these women's squalid existence. The speech made a strong impression, not only in the
House, but on the country at large. Legislation was passed,
prohibiting women from being employed underground;
and the same Bill made it illegal for children of ten and under
to be sent down the mines. Women still worked on the surface, however, and it was a good many years before the last
woman hauled her last truck of coal from the pit-head to the
wagons.

XIV

OUTSTANDING WOMEN

Caroline Chisholm, the "Emigrant's Friend"—Journey to Australia—The Home for Immigrant Women—Finding Wives for Settlers—The Family Colonization Loan Society. Mary Carpenter—Slum Children in Bristol— The First Reformatory School—"Juvenile Delinquents"—The First Youthful Offenders Act. Angela Burdett-Coutts—The Responsibilities of Great Wealth—The Scope of her Benefactions—Her Conception of Philanthropy

NEXT to Queen Victoria herself Florence Nightingale was probably the most outstanding woman of the Victorian Age. She would have been a powerfully outstanding person in any era, but the nineteenth century gave her the opportunities which she was peculiarly fitted to grasp. Her character and achievements have at last emerged from the legends which grew round her in her own lifetime, and the dramatized fictions which have diminished her in ours. An authentic life has at last been written—that by Mrs Woodham-Smith—and I hope it will be 'required reading' in schools in future.

Of the many lesser-known unusual women in the early part of Victoria's reign three stand out because of the unexpected character of their several achievements. The first was Caroline Chisholm; the second, Mary Carpenter; and the third, Angela Burdett-Coutts.

Caroline Chisholm took up the cause of the poor emigrant, and she was known as the "Emigrant's Friend." A letter was once actually sent to her addressed: "Mrs Chisholm, the Emigrant's Friend, England or Elsewhere," and was delivered at her house. The fact that she was so soon forgotten after her death is due to the chastening but inevitable fact that when pioneer work is at last recognized and incorporated into official procedure the name of the pioneer disappears. Not that Mrs Chisholm would have minded; it was the work itself that mattered to her, not the desire for praise.

She was born Caroline Jones, the daughter of a yeoman farmer, in 1808. Her father was a man of liberal ideas, with a turn for practical Christianity. He brought an old maimed soldier to live in his household, and the old man used to tell the children about lands far across the oceans—lands which were almost empty of people, but where the climate was good, food grew in abundance, and the prospect of wealth promising to those who would cross half the world and live there. These stories made an impression on Caroline. Warm-hearted by nature, she grew up with a strong missionary sense of being bound to help people; a feeling common to all the Victorian reformers, but especially marked in Caroline from her earliest years.

In 1830 she married Archibald Chisholm, a captain in the service of the East India Company, and went out with him to India two years later. Caroline soon found plenty to do. There were many young girls running wild at the station to which the Chisholms were posted: soldiers' daughters and orphans, exposed to the temptations of barrack-life for want of regular occupation. Mrs Chisholm started a school for them, where they were given a thorough domestic training, together with more formal education. The girls helped in the management of the school, which was run on lines which, even a hundred years later, would have been called progressive.

Captain Chisholm left India in 1838, and took his wife and family to Australia, settling in Sydney. Here Mrs Chisholm found girls in a worse plight than those she had helped in India. Emigration from England was in full spate, and thousands of young women had come to Australia. After scraping together enough money for the fare few of them had anything left over, and many were destitute within a few days of their arrival. At one time there were known to be six hundred of these young emigrants sleeping in recesses of the rocks along the shore, rather than encounter the dangers of the streets.

Mrs Chisholm began to rouse local opinion. The newspapers were helpful, and a committee of ladies was formed
with the object of agitating for a Home to be set up for
immigrant women to live in until they found situations. The
Governor of the colony regarded Mrs Chisholm as "a lady
labouring under amiable delusions," and when he at last
agreed to an interview with her expected her to talk to him
about his soul. He found instead, as he later described, "a
handsome, stately young woman, who proceeded to reason
the question as if she thought her reason, and experience,
too, worth as much as mine."

The Governor's wife was also impressed, and in the end
Caroline was given the use of part of a Government building, provided the authorities were not put to any expense
on account of her scheme. She at once set to work to make
this building habitable. It meant leaving her own cottage
and going to live in the Home itself—a great wrench, for
this meant separation from her children. There was no
other way of making the Home a success, and the sacrifice
was made. Soon a hundred girls were staying at the Home;
as they found situations others took their places. A new
problem presented itself. Women workers were needed
most up-country, and the young immigrants were afraid
to travel into the interior alone. Mrs Chisholm began to
take parties of girls out under her own protection, leaving
the Home to be managed by sympathizers who knew the
value of the work she had started.

Caroline Chisholm's journeys became legendary. She
travelled thousands of miles, going from settlement to
settlement, farm to farm, placing her charges in families
where she felt they would be safe and properly looked after.
She was asked many times to find lone settlers wives; she
relates in her memoirs how one man came to her camp with
a list of his possessions and a certificate of good character
from a magistrate, and said: "Come now, Mrs Chisholm,
do be a mother to me and get me a wife . . . have you not
got a nice girl from Tipperary? I should make a kind husband to one of your girls."

The majority of the immigrants did in fact marry; Mrs

CAROLINE CHISHOLM
From an engraving
By courtesy of the Women's Service Library

MARY CARPENTER
By courtesy of the "Illustrated London News"

ANGELA BURDETT-COUTTS

By courtesy of the "Illustrated London News"

Chisholm had letters from hundreds of them, blessing her for the help she had given them and saying how happy they were in their new lives.

The work expanded still further. Mrs Chisholm found herself escorting and settling immigrant men as well as women; and then she began to settle entire families, wherever she could. This was something that appealed to her most. Perhaps some memory of the old soldier's tales in her childhood lingered: here was one of the countries of which he had told her, where there were opportunities for all. What this huge, undeveloped land needed was populating— people making homes and rearing children. Mrs Chisholm turned her mind to the problem of getting men farms of their own, rather than situations as employees. There was one overriding difficulty: the colonial Government was prepared to sell land cheaply, but only in lots of three hundred acres or over. Few immigrants could afford anything like the sum required, £1 an acre. Mrs Chisholm persuaded several private owners of land to let the newcomers have holdings of twenty to forty acres, and the scheme turned out to be such a success that the Government reduced their minimum to fifty acres.

The work prospered. The people in the cities supported it as well as the settlers in the bush; wherever she went Mrs Chisholm was met with hospitality and a welcome for her protegés. By the time she had been in Australia seven years she had settled eleven thousand people in the colony of New South Wales.

Captain Chisholm had always encouraged her in her work, and when they prepared to return to England with their family in 1846 he accompanied her on a tour of the colony, where they travelled into remote regions, collecting all kinds of information which they thought would be useful to people in England who wanted to emigrate. Much of this information was written down in lonely farmsteads, or at the roadside as men worked, or in the fields with a plough serving as a desk.

There was deeply felt regret everywhere at their leaving the colony, but Mrs Chisholm had no intention of letting

L

her work drop. Once back in England, she began to give public talks on behalf of the thousands of men who had been transported to Australia for no very heinous crimes, who had been released there and were living in what she called a "demoralizing state of bachelorism." She was sure that they would turn into useful and hard-working citizens of the colony if their families were allowed to join them; otherwise, living alone, they would deteriorate and be like brutes.

Caroline Chisholm was not, by contemporary accounts, a forceful woman; but it is clear that she was single-minded when she felt a thing needed doing. Compassion is often as great a driving power as fanatical conviction. Mrs Chisholm had seen for herself how unhappy loneliness could make a man living thousands of miles away from his native land. She set to work to make other people realize it too. An open letter which she sent to the Emigration Commissioners said plainly that the men in the colonies needed their wives and children before they needed clergy, schoolmasters, churches, and books.

The Commissioners saw her personally and listened to her suggestion—that a grant of free passages should be made to the wives of convicts who held tickets-of-leave in New South Wales. She had already got a list of names, and an undertaking from the colony that not only were they willing to welcomes the wives, but were prepared to pay for the passages of children whose parents were already there. The scheme was agreed to, and Mrs Chisholm turned to the next part of her plan.

This was the formation of an information bureau for intending emigrants. The response was immediate; the rooms were crowded with people seeking advice. By 1852 she was receiving a thousand letters a week. Six clerks helped her with these—but she never delegated to others the duty of visiting the emigrant ships before they sailed, and seeing to every detail which would make the travellers comfortable for the voyage, and easy in their minds about the future.

Mrs Chisholm's next activity was the founding of a Family Colonization Loan Society, with whose help entire families were grouped together in small communities, and sent out to New South Wales as a unit. The families in each group undertook to repay the loans over a period of time, and to help each other if the need arose. This was one of the most imaginative of all Mrs Chisholm's schemes. Letters from Australia were published in newspapers and magazines at home, showing how heartfelt was the gratitude of the men and women who had been able to take their families out to a new country, knowing that they had work waiting for them and friends to whom they could turn.

Caroline Chisholm died in 1877. By that time the colonial Governments in Australia had established Homes for immigrants, the transportation system had been abolished, and there was abundant official assistance for men and women with small means who wanted to settle in the country. All Mrs Chisholm's work was gradually taken over and incorporated into the emigration system.

She was not a spectacular figure. But she helped thousands of people to a decent and self-respecting way of living, and it is good to know that she was honoured in her lifetime. Robert Lowe, a member of the Legislature of New South Wales, said of her:

"One person only in the colony has done anything effectual . . . to mitigate this crying evil and national sin, and to fix *families* on our lands in lieu of bachelors. And . . . that one is a humble, unpretending, quiet-working female missionary! an emigrant missionary, not a clerical one! The singularity of her mission is one of the most original that was ever devised or undertaken by either man or woman; and the object, the labour, the design are beyond all praise."

To turn from Caroline Chisholm and her singular mission to Mary Carpenter and her work among the ragged children of Bristol is to enter the more familiar field of social service among the poor. But Mary Carpenter was no ordinary social worker, and she initiated reforms and familiarized a phrase which are as much in the public mind to-day as they were a hundred years ago. When one comes across an article in a woman's periodical headed "Juvenile Delinquency" it takes a minute or two to realize that the date is 1853 and not the present year.

Mary Carpenter was born in Devonshire in 1807, the daughter of a minister who was also a schoolmaster. Brought up in an atmosphere of piety and philanthropy, she was helping her parents with their various forms of social work well before she was out of her teens. She also assisted her mother with a girls' school which Mrs Carpenter kept.

Bristol, with its docks and mean streets behind the wharves, had a large slum population, and Mary founded a "working and visiting society" for helping the poor. An encounter with a ragged child opened her eyes to the dangers which surrounded these wild slum children, and she opened a school for them in one of the worst districts of Bristol. Ragged schools were not unknown at that period, but Mary Carpenter's methods of conducting such a school were new. She tried two weapons which had rarely been used before: patience and kindness. The result at first was bedlam. The children behaved like little animals, breaking windows and furniture, tearing up books and papers. Mary Carpenter laid out a playground where they could rush about and work off their energy, and gradually some order came into being inside the school.

Mary had thought a good deal about the problem of slum children being turned by force of circumstances into potential young criminals. She believed that preventive work was more likely to be effective than punitive measures after a young person had actually committed a crime. In 1851 she published her views in a book: *Reformatory Schools, for the Children of the Perishing and Dangerous Classes, and for Juvenile Offenders*. The book roused much interest; there were reviews in local papers throughout the country, as well as in the national journals. A notice in *La Belle Assemblée* in 1852 said:

"Crime is not, as many suppose, a *lawless* thing; it grows up and flourishes under certain conditions, and if these are changed it is modified in its form, or it altogether disappears. No remedy is worth applying unless it go to the root of the matter. Crimes against prosperity are the most common in our state of society, and this is sure to be the case in all communities where there is much wealth on one side, and much poverty and ignorance on the other. Ignorance is a great feeder of crime; it is this that prevents the criminal from seeing the consequences of his act. . . . Ignorance is, in a certain sense, not so much an index of crime as the very element in which it grows, and it would go some considerable way to lessen crime were ignorance made less common than unfortunately it is. The amiable author of the work now before us has paid much attention to the mutual relations subsisting between crime and education, and she purposes 'Reformatory Schools' for children of a certain age who have once subjected themselves to the severity of the law."

The reviewer went on to talk of the "short-sighted economy that prevents the people of England from securing to every English child the rudiments of letters; if they will not help the *falling*, how can we expect them to do anything for the *fallen* but trample on them?" Miss Carpenter was not to lose heart if Society did not at once respond to her arguments, but, ended the reviewer, "let her call and call again, and by her continual coming she will weary them."

Mary Carpenter had every intention of calling and calling again. She put forward her ideas clearly and earnestly before a Parliamentary committee inquiring into juvenile delinquency, and she opened her own 'reformatory school,' based on the principles she had worked out. Another book, *Juvenile Delinquents, their Condition and Treatment*, followed in 1853, and was equally well received.

One of the first-fruits of her labours was the passing of the Youthful Offenders Act (1854) which legalized the position of new reformatory schools on the model she had laid down. She opened a separate school for girls at Red Lodge, in Park Row, Bristol—the house where Frances Power Cobbe helped her for some time. Miss Cobbe, in her *Life*, draws an unforgettable picture of Mary Carpenter at this time: austere, completely selfless, and devoted to the work she had undertaken.

Mary Carpenter now tried to get a share of State education for her schools, and urged Members of Parliament to support the Industrial Schools Bill, which would enable ragged schools to participate in the educational grant. The Bill was passed in 1857, but there were many difficulties in the way of its full implementation. So this singular woman opened an industrial school herself, to show the authorities in practical fashion how badly reforms were needed. Many of her proposals were adopted as amendments to later Acts.

Her further work lies outside our period. She had become interested in Indian problems of education and prison reform, and travelled to India in later years to advise on these questions; she also went to the United States and Canada. It is her middle years which concern us here, the years of experiment outside the path of conventional good works. Mary Carpenter used her brain as well as her heart; her natural benevolence was strengthened by a genuine understanding of the "perishing classes" of her day.

The treatment of juvenile delinquency has become a social science, and reformatory schools are now outdated. But behind every probation officer, every humanitarian magistrate sitting in a children's court, there is the spirit of Mary Carpenter, a spirit which believes that discipline should be, not punitive, but—in Miss Carpenter's own word—"restorative."

Philanthropy, in many forms, was one of the strong impulses of the Victorian Age, and there were many women philanthropists who spent their time and money relieving the needs of the unfortunate. But one of them stood apart from the rest, both by reason of her personality and the scale on which she exercised her philanthropy. Angela Burdett-Coutts was unique.

Born in 1814, Angela Burdett was the youngest child of Sir Francis Burdett, a politician conspicuous for his advanced opinions on most of the controversial subjects of his time. He supported Parliamentary reform, prison reform, Catholic Emancipation, and other radical measures. An attack by him on the conduct of the House of Commons ended in his imprisonment in the Tower on one occasion. He married the daughter of Thomas Coutts, the banker, and Angela was their youngest child. Intelligent, sensible, endowed with grace and dignity, Angela travelled abroad, met many of the most distinguished men and women of letters and science, and was one of the best-educated girls of her class and generation.

Thomas Coutts was enormously wealthy when he died. He left his fortune to his second wife, the actress Harriet Mellon, who later married into the peerage, and is referred to in contemporary letters as the "old Duchess." Harriet recognized character when she met it, and she left the Coutts riches to her youngest step-grandchild. At the age of twenty-three Angela Burdett was the richest heiress in England. There were many fortune-hunters after this prize, but Angela refused matrimony, and proceeded to set up her own establishment. She added her grandfather's name to her own, and soon Miss Burdett-Coutts was entertaining notabilities from home and abroad: scholars, musicians, actors, statesmen. Her interests spread far round her; she had a real desire to understand the world in which she lived —and this inevitably led her to a study of the appalling social conditions of the time.

It would have been easy for her to give sums of money to worthy objects, as was the usual practice of the rich. Angela Burdett-Coutts had a more serious conception of the responsibilities of giving. She had inherited her grandfather's business capacity as well as his wealth, and she took an active part in the administration of her fortune, studying all the demands made on her charity with penetrating attention. One of the close friends she made was Charles Dickens, who helped her over a long period to plan her benefactions. These form an astonishing list—astonishing not only in length, but in scope. From the middle of the nineteenth century to the date of her death, in 1906, she spent great sums of money for the public good. She built churches and schools, model blocks of dwellings, and clubs for poverty-stricken youth. She endowed bishoprics in South Africa and Australia, established sewing-schools for girls in the

East End of London, gathered street-arabs into a "shoe-black's brigade" so that they could earn a living, founded friendly societies and working-men's societies—and was generally ready to help those who made some effort to help themselves.

Discriminating, quietly strong-willed, Angela Burdett-Coutts lived through the long Victorian scene without being in the least changed by the great power which her wealth brought her. She was a perpetual reminder to both the feminists and the anti-feminists that a young woman could have every ladylike accomplishment, charm, and a good figure, and be capable of conducting a complex of financial activities with a masculine wisdom and assurance.

XV

TOWARDS EMANCIPATION

The Women's Movement—The Lack of Civil Rights—The Fear of Female Domination—Anti-feminists—Caroline Norton—The Infant Custody Bill—Barbara Leigh Smith—A Pamphlet on Laws affecting Women—Petitions to Parliament—Elizabeth Blackwell—The Hope for the Future

THE Women's Movement, as it was called in the nineteenth century, might be said to have begun with Mary Wollstonecraft's *A Vindication of the Rights of Woman*, which brought its author ridicule and contempt in her lifetime, but which was to have a far-reaching influence on the women who came after her.

There were "Female Reformers" in the first two decades of the century, but they were associations of working women whose objects were to help their menfolk achieve some measure of reform in general social conditions; they were not feminists in the later sense of the word.

At least two of the champions of women's political rights were men: John Stuart Mill, whose famous *Subjection of Women* was published in the sixties; less well-known was William Thompson of Cork, who had written a book in 1825 called *Appeal of One Half of the Human Race, Women, against the Pretensions of the Other Half, Men.* Thompson contended that there would be no human progress until women were given equal opportunities for education and equal political rights with men. His arguments were clear and cogent, and though there is no evidence that he was widely read, he undoubtedly influenced writers like Mrs Hugo Reid, who was developing the same theme in the next decade.

In her *Plea for Woman*, mentioned in a previous chapter, Mrs Reid insisted that the granting of ordinary civil rights

to women need in no way interfere with their domestic
relationships, and that they were not bound to lose their
grace and womanly qualities if they exercised their intellect
and judgment. She said:

"The consciousness of responsibility which the posession
of a vote would bestow, the dignity of being trusted, the
resolution to justify the faith placed in her truth and judgment, would all call forth . . . powers which, hitherto, have
been too much suffered to lie dormant."

She went on to castigate those contemporaries who took
the line of least resistance and encouraged others to do the
same:

"Some . . . gifted women have been induced to hide
their light beneath an exterior of levity and frivolity, while
others have gained the pardon of the lord of creation for
encroaching on what he claims as his peculiar domain—the
intellectual—by falling down and worshipping him, and
then devoting their talents to instructing their sex in all the
duties of this idolatry."

Putting forward the daring claim, not only to vote, but
to be represented in Parliament by her own sex, Mrs Reid
pointed out that unless women could be so represented,
there was little chance of the laws which pressed so hardly
on them being changed. She rejected men's fear of female
domination as she rejected the other objection which was
constantly being put forward—that the introduction of
women into public life would injure their gentleness and
modesty. She asked:

"Are the business habits [of men] so rough that they are
afraid to allow of women mingling with them, lest they
should . . . become as uncouth . . . as themselves? Why!
let them mend their manners, and the difficulty at once
disappears. . . .

"Subjects must sometimes come under discussion [in
Parliament] 'which could not be mooted before a female
audience without shocking that nice sense of decorum which
no right-minded person can wish to render less sensitive.' We
suppose that the above alludes to those terrible disorders
and desperate vices of society, a fearful and shuddering

glimpse of which is all that her own ideas of propriety allow to a modest woman; and, if such be the case ... a better acquaintance with those dreadful evils, and even great efforts to amend them, are perfectly consistent with female delicacy: to the pure all things are pure. The possession of a truer and more complete knowledge on this painful subject, by women in general, would do more to lessen the numbers of the most unfortunate outcasts of society— many of them more sinned against than sinning—than all the secret discussions of the House of Commons."

It was brave of Mrs Reid even to hint in her book at the subject of prostitution, which was one of the most terrible problems of the whole Victorian era. Josephine Butler had not yet begun her courageous pioneer work in this field; she married in 1852, and it was nearly fifteen years after that before she started on her mission of helping the fallen women of Liverpool, thereafter devoting her life to the fight against organized vice which was to startle and horrify the late Victorian world. In the forties and fifties the subject was taboo in polite society; any reference to it had to be made with extreme caution, exemplified in this letter in a woman's journal of 1845. The extract begins:

"Apropos of the midnight meeting of the erring sisterhood at St James' Restaurant, An Englishwoman makes this proposal:

"'Might I venture to suggest that a meeting be called of the other sex, that they might be lectured and prayed with about the awful sin and misery that lie at their door? I will bear my share of the necessary tea and toast. When the demand ceases the supply will soon be stopped.'"

But to return to Mrs Hugo Reid. She, and those who thought like her, put forward cool arguments; the opposition answered with abuse and emotional tirades. From the Queen downward—Victoria thought the emancipation movement "wicked"—there were violent protests against females wanting to be considered as citizens as well as wives and daughters. S. C. Hall, the editor of the *New Monthly Magazine*, fought the idea with tongue and pen, and used his influence at every opportunity to discredit any writer or figure in public life who encouraged what he called "these foolish brawlers." His wife, the novelist Anna Maria Hall, was as fanatically anti-feminist, and her diatribe in her husband's *Book of Memories* is worth quoting if only because it is typical of the general attitude towards the women of that time who were struggling for reasonable conditions of living:

"It is a matter for deep regret, for intense sorrow, indeed, that women have recently inaugurated a movement for what they call the creation of 'Women's Rights.'. . . I believe this movement to be pregnant with incalculable danger to men, but especially to women. . . . Electoral rights would deprive them of their power and lower their position under a pretence to raise it. I warn all women of all countries, all ages, all conditions, all classes! And I humbly urge upon the Legislature to resist demands that are opposed to Wisdom, Mercy, and Religion.

"Women may cease to be women, as regards all that makes them most attractive . . . it is surely mental blindness which cannot foresee the misery that must follow the altered relations and changed conditions of both men and women. . . . I am quite sure the guiding and controlling impulse of women is to render themselves agreeable and helpful to men. . . . An unwomanly woman is always avoided; a masculine woman is more repulsive than an effeminate man. . . . No doubt some designing, or ambitious, or 'unsexed' women, self-appointed leaders, have led weak women to follow them—sheep gone astray. The number is small, but it may be augmented by ignorance and prejudice. . . .

"It is no exaggeration to say that 'those who rock the cradle rule the world.' The future rests mainly with the mother; foolish are all who strive for the enactment of laws that would deprive her of her holiest rights, to try a wild experiment by which, under the senseless cry of 'equality,' women would be displaced from the position in which God has placed them since the beginning of the world, for all Time, and for Eternity."

Mrs Hall's idyllic picture of the mother rocking the

cradle was calculated to appeal to the strongest instincts in that home-loving era, but the appeal had a double edge. Many women reading those words must have remembered in the same moment that a woman had no legal right whatever to either the cradle she was rocking or to its occupant.[1] If her husband chose to desert her he could take her baby away to be brought up by his mistress, and she, the mother, would have no redress.

It was to try to get iniquitous laws of this kind altered that spurred so many women on to agitate for political rights. Every one knew that the laws affecting women were unjust, and many people deplored them; but the general attitude was that most marriages rested on a solid foundation of mutual trust and affection, and to make special laws for the protection of wives would cast a slur on the institution of matrimony.

The first attack on this attitude of complacency was made by a woman much in the public eye, Caroline Norton. She was a fashionable writer, and her matrimonial troubles had been publicized for years. She was no supporter of the "Women's Movement"; her rebellion against the existing laws affecting married women was inspired by a furious resentment that her worthless husband should be able to treat her with injustice and still have the law on his side.

Caroline, a granddaughter of Richard Brinsley Sheridan, married the Hon. George Norton in 1827. She was nineteen; a great beauty, impulsive, talented, with a literary reputation already made. She was also a brilliant social success, an acknowledged ornament in artistic as well as political circles. She was not in love with Norton. She married him because, in the words of her biographer, "she was now in the classic dilemma of her class and generation . . . she knew well that she had to marry. In the eyes of her contemporaries she could count herself lucky that a moderately eligible bachelor was sufficiently in love with her to overlook her lack of dowry." It was an unhappy marriage. Norton turned out to be weak, spiteful, mean about money, obstinate. They quarrelled continually, and there were

[1] See footnote at p. 26.

constant scenes. Norton had violent outbursts of rage, and even attacked Caroline with physical force.

Three children were born of the marriage—all sons—and it is clear that George Norton cared for his boys and that they could have been a stabilizing factor in the marriage. But the temperaments of husband and wife were too much opposed. Caroline had inherited the Sheridan independence and high temper, and on several occasions she left the house and took refuge with her mother and sisters. She returned because she could not take the children with her; and because, too, George Norton was constantly in money difficulties, and Caroline was earning substantial sums from her literary work, money which she was always willing to spend on household expenses.

Their stormy married life went on. Caroline found relief in her writing and in the many friendships which she made in society. She had long been friendly with Lord Melbourne, then middle-aged, but a person very much like herself—talented, attractive, sympathetic. It was an innocent friendship, a fact which George Norton very well knew; but it could be made to look less innocent. At the end of 1835, when Caroline was visiting her relations after a painful quarrel with her husband, Norton sent the children away to stay with his cousin, who refused to allow Caroline to see them. Norton then brought an action against Lord Melbourne for "criminal conversation" with his wife. It was a farcical case. There was no real evidence at all, and the case was dismissed. But though Caroline cleared her reputation, she soon learned to what misery her husband's spite could bring her. He sent the children right away, so that she did not know where they were; he refused to support her, and claimed her possessions as his own—a claim which he could enforce by law.

Caroline was almost penniless, but she had a staunch family behind her, loyal friends, and a public. She began to write pamphlets, which she had privately printed and circulated among the most influential people of the day. *The Natural Claim of a Mother to the Custody of her Child as affected by the Common Law Right of the Father* was printed in 1837, and contained evidence which she had collected of cases which were even worse than her own.

Her object was no less than to try to get the law changed, and she pursued this aim with all her passion and energy. She realized that she had no chance of regaining her children with the law as it stood. Her chief hope lay in a clever young barrister, Serjeant Talfourd, who had been one of the counsel for Melbourne at the trial, and who was also a Member of Parliament. Talfourd, a man of progressive outlook, had for long been disturbed by the terrible cases of misery and injustice in the courts, where he had seen badly treated wives deprived of their children through no fault of their own. Before he had ever met Mrs Norton or heard of her case he had decided to introduce an Infants' Custody Bill into Parliament. He now put it forward. The Bill had a stormy passage; it passed the Commons, but was thrown out when it reached the Lords. Caroline was not disheartened, and when the Bill was later reintroduced, she canvassed all her political friends for its support. It passed the Commons once more, and in 1839 reached the Lords again. Caroline knew now that she had enemies as well as friends in the Upper Chamber, and she determined to try to get the Lords to consider the Bill objectively. She wrote a pamphlet, *A Plain Letter to the Lord Chancellor on the Infant Custody Bill*, signed it with a masculine name, because she thought that would carry more weight, and sent it to every peer. Its logical presentation of facts and clear arguments had the effect Caroline had hoped for; the Lords passed the Bill, and at last it became law.

Caroline Norton had troubles enough after that first victory. The struggle for her children was to go on for a long time, and she was to know the grief of losing one of them before she finally won her fight. But it was that first victory which counted for much in the slow and determined movement of the women of her time towards emancipation. She was the first woman to challenge successfully the power of the law, and the fact that she did so for personal reasons, and used her social and political influence to help her, did not detract from her achievement.

*   *   *   *   *

Barbara Leigh Smith, who later became Madame Bodichon, was a rebel of an entirely different kind; a disinterested rebel from the point of view of her private life, but a most forceful and determined one by virtue of a temperament which strongly resented injustice.

This young reformer was fortunate in her own nature and in her family. She was born in 1827, the eldest daughter of Benjamin Smith, a Radical member of Parliament. Barbara grew up in an atmosphere of liberal ideas; she met most of the reformers and serious writers of the day, and developed into a young woman of high intelligence and quick, warm sympathies. She also possessed something that was quite unique for a girl—an income of her own. It had been settled on her when she came of age; Benjamin Smith believed in treating his sons and daughters alike. Barbara had always taken such equality for granted at home, but by the time she was twenty, and had met people from backgrounds other than her own, she realized how lucky she was. Few girls were given more than a dress allowance and pin-money for charitable purposes, unless they were heiresses in their own right. The married woman, Barbara discovered, was in worse case. She had no money at all in her own right. A single girl could at least own property or money, if she had any; but if she married, everything passed at once into the possession of her husband, and she no longer even owned the clothes she stood up in. That was the law.

It is not quite clear what decided Barbara Leigh Smith to begin a campaign against the existing laws of property. She was possibly influenced by the zeal for reform which was the spiritual climate in which she had grown up. Perhaps she was stimulated by what she had heard of Caroline Norton; her father knew Serjeant Talfourd, and it is likely that the inequalities and shortcomings of the existing laws were discussed in that household, where social questions were considered of importance to young minds as well as to old. The fact remains that Barbara did make the decision to do something, and she set about it in her own individual way.

First she studied the laws which affected women, and

THE EFFICIENCY OF FEMALE POLICE IN WHAT IS VULGARLY
CALLED A "JOLLY ROW"

J. Leech (from *Punch's Almanack*)

Reproduced by permission of the Proprietors of "Punch"

THE VOLUNTEER MOVEMENT: JONES AND FAMILY GO
UNDER CANVAS

J. Leech

From the author's collection

THE PROGRESS OF BLOOMERISM

"It's a very strange thing, Harry, that with so many brothers I never have a button on my collars. . . ."

"Now, you know, Miss Charlotte, your Pa won't have no smoking in the nursery."

"But I say, Ma dear, I may call at Tattersall's . . . I want to buy a cob . . ."

J. Leech

From the author's collection

THE BARRISTER

J. Leech (from *Punch's Almanack*)

Reproduced by permission of the Proprietors of "Punch"

selected those which she thought the most important. Then
she wrote a pamphlet which she called: *A Brief Summary in
Plain Language of the Most Important Laws concerning Women*.
It was published in 1854, and at once attracted attention. I
have a copy of the pamphlet before me as I write. It is a
model of conciseness and clarity: a lawyer could hardly
have set out a case more tellingly. Barbara indulged in no
irrelevancies, no emotional appeals. She put down plain
facts, beginning with the legal conditions of spinsters; their
rights to property and to protection from the law; their
position as heirs; their powers to vote upon parish questions, but not for Members of Parliament; the limitations
imposed upon them regarding employment.

Then came the laws concerning married women; a long
list, including those concerning a husband's absolute rights
over his wife's property and earnings, whether she was
living with him or not. Barbara had discovered that a man
actually had a legal right to the property of his *betrothed* wife,
who could not dispose of her property without his knowledge, once she had given him a promise of marriage. After
listing the laws of separation and divorce, and those affecting widows and unmarried mothers, Barbara added a few
pages headed "Remarks." She compared the position of
married women in England with that held by women in
France, Hungary, and Germany, pointing out that in those
countries, and in some of the American states, women were
able to own and dispose of their property whether they were
married or not. She asked for the abolition of a law which
had been outgrown in her own country, and ended: "We
do not say that these laws of property are the only unjust
laws concerning women to be found in the short summary
which we have given, but they form a simple, tangible,
and not offensive point of attack."

The last sentence was characteristic of its writer; she
believed that a reasonable statement of conditions not sufficiently known would be enough to bring about a reform.
She was to learn many lessons on that point.

The pamphlet was put before the Law Amendment
Society, a body which included some of the most eminent

M

legal men of the time. They were impressed by its exposition, and a few months later drafted a report which proposed giving married women rights in their own property. Meetings were held and petitions were drawn up, supporting the proposed amendment of the law; over 25,000 men and women signed the petitions, which were taken to Parliament. A Bill was put before the Commons, and passed its second reading, but its fortunes were halted by another Bill which had just been introduced. This was the Marriage and Divorce Bill, designed to make divorce a law courts procedure, instead of being possible only through Act of Parliament or the ecclesiastical courts.

There was more heat than light engendered over these two important Bills affecting women. The full force of Victorian moral indignation in its worse aspects was let loose in pamphlets and articles. The home was being attacked: marriage was being attacked: the foundations of society were being attacked: religion was being attacked. The reforming element was equally articulate. Had not the time come for these age-old abuses to be remedied? Was this not a civilized country? Was one half of the human race to be denied elementary justice and kept in perpetual subjection?

Among people in public life with opinions on the subject was the middle-aged Mr Gladstone, who delivered long speeches against the Bill. A well-known personage from a previous decade stepped again into the limelight in support of the Bill: Caroline Norton. She had reason enough to know how hardly the marriage laws pressed upon wives. Mrs Norton was not concerned now, any more than she had been before, with women's political equality. She wanted three amendments inserted into the new Bill: one, that a man could not claim the earnings of the wife he had deserted; two, that a separated or divorced wife could inherit or bequeath property; and three, that such a woman could have the power to sue or be sued apart from her husband, thus giving her a legal entity.

The amendments were incorporated in the new Bill, which was passed in 1857. Barbara Leigh Smith and her friends realized that their separate Bill would have no chance of success, now that the worst abuses regarding a deserted wife's property had been dealt with in the new Act. Their Bill got no farther, but agitation for fuller reforms went on. They had planted seeds which were to grow.

The *Ladies' Newspaper* for February 23, 1856, contained this item:

"REVOLUTION IN SCIENCE. A lady, the daughter of the late Samuel Blackwell, of Bristol, has just completed her medical studies in Paris, and obtained a diploma to practise as a physician. She has a sister, who pursued her studies also in Paris, who is acting in a similar capacity under the title of Dr Elizabeth Blackwell. The lady who has just obtained this honourable distinction is Dr Emily Blackwell. Her studies have been principally directed to the diseases of women and children."

Emily Blackwell's achievement, fine as it was, hardly merited the heading to the news-item; she had but followed in her sister's footsteps. It was Elizabeth who had caused the revolution in science when she qualified for a medical degree seven years earlier, and began to practise in New York. It is clear from Elizabeth Blackwell's own account of her early days that she was not a born doctor, as some women are born nurses. A chance circumstance decided her to leave the comparative security of her life at home and turn to the hazards of attempting to enter a profession which until then had been closed to women in America as well as in England.

Elizabeth Blackwell was born in Bristol in 1821, the third daughter of nine children. When she was eleven years old her father, a business-man, emigrated with his family to America. Samuel Blackwell died less than a year later, and the elder daughters had to teach until such time as their brothers were old enough to contribute towards the household. Elizabeth was a young woman of character, with a taste for study. One of her friends, an invalid who suffered from a painful disease, said to her one day: "Why not study medicine? If I could have been treated by a lady

doctor my worst sufferings would have been spared me."
Elizabeth then saw that many women hesitated to go to
doctors because of the intimate nature of their complaints.

The idea of women doctors began to take hold of her.
She had a natural revulsion from the prospect of a medical
training for herself, but she overcame that by will-power.
It now seemed to her very important that women should
be able to enter the medical profession. After a good deal of
thought she resolved to open the way in America, if she
could, for women to study medicine on the same terms as
men. She knew that she would need a large amount of
money, and she taught in school by day and did what studying she could in the evenings. Her family helped and encouraged her, and she was able to save enough money to
justify her seeking admission to a medical school.

Her applications to the principal colleges with faculties
of medicine in Philadelphia were refused. The dean of one
college said to her: "You cannot expect us to furnish you
with a stick to break our heads with." Elizabeth had
expected opposition. She sent applications to other schools
in the northern states. At last, after about a dozen refusals,
she received a letter from the medical school at Geneva,
in New York State, accepting her. The faculty there had
taken the sensible course of putting her application before
the students, who had replied, after consulting among
themselves, that "one of the radical principles of a Republi-
can government is the universal education of both sexes;
that to every branch of scientific education the door should
be open equally to all; that the application of Elizabeth
Blackwell to become a member of our class meets with our
entire approbation." They also promised to behave themselves in the presence of a lady. Elizabeth later paid tribute
to the courteous treatment she received from them. The
people who were rude to her were members of her own sex
outside the college—"with shocked propriety they glared
at me as I passed."

After two years at Geneva Elizabeth walked the wards of
a hospital in Philadelphia, and at the end of a further period
of study at her college qualified as a medical practitioner in

1849. The American Press was neither facetious nor patronizing; it recognized her achievement and commented favourably upon it. Other women began to follow her example, among them being her sister Emily.

Soon after she qualified Elizabeth Blackwell came to Europe. She spent some months at the famous La Maternité Hospital, in Paris. One wonders if she ever thought of her reply to a doctor who had, in America, advised her against going to Paris and seeing the horrors there: "If the path of duty led me to hell I would go there."

She also came to London, and was accepted for a course of study at St Bartholomew's Hospital. She was accepted because she was already a qualified doctor. Women were not admitted as medical students to any English hospital or university. In London Dr Blackwell met Barbara Leigh Smith, Florence Nightingale, and many of the distinguished men and women in scientific and liberal-minded society. She and Miss Nightingale became friends; it was before Florence Nightingale had finally broken away from the empty social existence which so galled her. Dr Blackwell relates how Miss Nightingale, escorted by a footman, would call on her in her lodgings, and how they would sit toasting their toes in front of the fire and talking. Most of the conversation seems to have been about sanitation. It was a subject which had a very real and terrible significance at that time, and both women were later to press home its importance in their different spheres.

Dr Blackwell returned to America in 1851, and founded a dispensary in New York which was to develop into the first hospital to be staffed by women doctors. Seven years later she visited England again, and though this date brings us beyond our period, it is worth continuing with her story in order to show the great influence she had on the women pioneers in medicine who tried to enter the profession in England.

In 1859 Dr Blackwell gave a series of lectures in London in which she described the work of women doctors in America. Elizabeth Garrett, later to become Mrs Garrett Anderson, was one of her listeners; Dr Blackwell described her as a "bright, intelligent young lady whose interest in the study of medicine was aroused."

In that same year Dr Blackwell was entered on the British Medical Register as the first qualified woman doctor in Great Britain. She was just in time. The authorities could not refuse to enter her name, even though she was a woman; any doctor with a foreign medical degree who had practised medicine was entitled to registration in Britain. In the following year doctors who held *only* foreign degrees were excluded from the Register—though such doctors as had been admitted already were not removed from it. The new charter which came into force laid down that a medical practitioner must have a British degree in order to practise.

The effect of this new provision was to take away all hope from women who had intended to follow Elizabeth Blackwell's example. Even if they qualified abroad they would not be allowed to practise in England.

That was the position when Dr Blackwell returned to New York in 1859, and it did not alter for many years. But Elizabeth Blackwell had taken women a step farther on the road to emancipation, for she had inspired the "bright, intelligent young lady" to go on with the fight against hostility and prejudice in the profession she wished to enter.

And so to the end of the fifties and the beginning of a new phase in the life of the nineteenth-century woman. Outwardly, existence followed its normal course. The crinoline gave way to the bustle, the bonnet to the feathered hat. Regency elegance disappeared under plush and fringe indoors, and foliated ironwork outdoors. But there was a change. Ideas were changing. Conventions were being challenged and superstitions ignored; a good education for girls was becoming a possibility. The mid-Victorian woman inherited a few rights and privileges which had been hard won by the rebels of her mother's generation. She herself was to encounter new conventions, fresh prejudices. But, like the early Victorian woman in whose steps she followed, she "received aliment and impulse from the very circumstances which would seem the most calculated to narrow and bind her."

SELECT BIBLIOGRAPHY

ACLAND, ALICE: *Caroline Norton* (Constable, 1948).

ACTON, ELIZA: *Modern Cookery in all its Branches* (1845).

ANONYMOUS: *The English Maiden: her Moral and Domestic Duties* (1841).

——:*The English Wife, a Manual of Home Duties* (1843).

——:*Female Piety: or, The Young Woman's Friend and Guide through Life to Immortality* (1853).

——: *The Girl's Own Book* (1848).

——: *Home Truths for Home Peace, or Muddle Defeated* (1852).

——: *Household Book of Domestic Economy* (1850).

——: *The Ladies' Pocket Book of Etiquette* (1840).

——: *Men's Duties to Women* (1852).

——:*Woman's Worth, or, Hints to raise the Female Character* (1844).

——: *The Young Lady's Friend*, by a Lady (1837).

BLACKSTONE, SIR WILLIAM: *Commentaries on the Law of England* (1765–69).

BROWNING, ELIZABETH BARRETT: *Letters*, edited by Frederic G. Kenyon (Smith and Elder, 1897).

BURTON, HESTER: *Barbara Bodichon* (Murray, 1949).

BUTLER, WILLIAM: *Exercises on the Globes* (1798).

CARLYLE, JANE WELSH: *Letters and Memorials*, edited by J. A. Froude (Longmans, 1883).

COBBE, FRANCES POWER: *Life*, by Herself (Bentley, 1894).

DAVIES, EMILY: *The Higher Education of Women* (Alexander Strahan, 1866).

ELLIS, SARAH: *The Women of England* (1838; sixteenth edition, 1841).

ENGELS, FRIEDRICH: *The Condition of the Working-class in England in 1844* (1892).

FONTANE, THEODOR: *Journeys to England in Victoria's Early Days: 1844–59*, translated by Dorothy Harrison (Massie, 1939).

FRANCATELLI, CHARLES ELMÉ: *A Plain Cookery Book for the Working-classes* (1861).

FRY, KATHERINE, AND CRESSWELL, R. E.: *Memoirs of the Life of Elizabeth Fry* (2 vols. 1847).

GRANVILLE, A. B.: *The Spas of England and Principal Sea-bathing Places* (1841).

GREVILLE, CHARLES: *The Greville Memoirs*, edited by H. Reeve (1875–87).

HAGGARD, H. W.: *Devils, Drugs, and Doctors* (Heinemann, 1929).

HALDANE, ELIZABETH: *Mrs Gaskell and her Friends* (Hodder and Stoughton 1930).

HALE, SARAH JOSEPHA: *Women's Record: or, Sketches of All Distinguished Women, from "The Beginning" till* A.D. *1850, arranged in Four Eras* (New York, 1853).

HALL, S. C.: *A Book of Memories of Great Men and Women of the Age, from Personal Acquaintance* (1871).

HAMMOND, J. L. AND BARBARA: *The Bleak Age* (Longmans, 1934).

HARRIS, H. WILSON: *Caroline Fox* (Constable, 1944).

KEMBLE, FRANCES A.: *Records of Later Life* (Bentley, 1882).

KITCHINER, DR WILLIAM: *The Cook's Oracle* (third edition, 1821, "almost entirely re-written").

LAVER, JAMES: *Taste and Fashion* (Harrap, 1945).

LUCKCOCK, JAMES: *Hints for Practical Economy in the Management of Household Affairs* (1834).

MACKENZIE, ENEAS: *Memoirs of Mrs Caroline Chisholm, with an Account of her Philanthropic Labours in India, Australia, and England* (1852).

MANGNALL, RICHMAL: *Historical and Miscellaneous Questions* (1800; successive editions up to 1860).

MARTINEAU, HARRIET: *Autobiography* (1877).

——: *Guides to Service* (1838).

——: *The Maid of All Work* (1838).

MAXWELL, CHRISTABEL: *Mrs Gatty and Mrs Ewing* (Constable, 1949).

MAYHEW, HENRY: *London Labour and the London Poor* (1861).

MILL, JOHN STUART: *The Subjection of Women* (1869).

MOORE, DORIS LANGLEY: *The Woman in Fashion* (Batsford, 1949).

NEFF, WANDA F.: *Victorian Working Women*, 1832–50 (Allen and Unwin, 1929).

NEVILL, LADY DOROTHY: *Under Five Reigns*, edited by Ralph Nevill (Methuen, 1912).

PARDOE, JULIA: *The Beauties of the Bosphorus* (1839).

PARKES, MRS WILLIAM: *Domestic Duties, or, Instructions to Young Married Ladies on the Management of their Households and the Regulation of their Conduct in the Various Relations and Duties of Married Life* (1825).

PRATT, E. A.: *Pioneer Women in Victoria's Reign* (Newnes, 1897).

RATCLIFFE, MRS: *The Young Woman's Companion: being a Complete Guide to Every Acquirement Essential in Forming a Useful Member of Society* (1843).

REID, MRS HUGO: *A Plea for Woman: being a Vindication of the Importance and Extent of her Natural Sphere of Action* (1843).

RUNDELL, MRS: *A New System of Domestic Cookery* (1819).

SMITH, BARBARA LEIGH: (Madame Bodichon): *A Brief Summary in Plain Language of the Most Important Laws of England Concerning Women* (first edition published anonymously in 1854).

SOYER, ALEXIS BENÔIT: *The Gastronomic Regenerator* (1846).

——: *The Modern Housewife, or Ménagère* (1849).

SPEAIGHT, GEORGE: *Juvenile Drama* (Macdonald, 1946).

STODART, M. A.: *Female Writers: Thoughts on their Proper Sphere, and on their Powers of Usefulness* (1842).

THACKERAY, W. M.: *Mr Brown's Letters to a Young Man about Town* (New York, 1853).

TODD, REV. JOHN: *The Daughter at School* (1854).

TRAILL, H. D., AND MANN, J. S.: *Social England*, vol. vi, 1815–85 (Cassell, 1904).

TROLLOPE, ANTHONY: *Autobiography* (Blackwood, 1883).

TUKE, DAME MARGARET: *A History of Bedford College for Women* (Oxford University Press, 1939).

TWEEDIE, MRS ALEC (ed.): *The First College for Women* (*Queen's College, Harley Street*) *1848–98* (Jubilee book published for the College, 1899).

WARD, MRS R.: *The Child's Guide to Knowledge*, by a Lady (second edition, 1828; more than forty later editions).

WEETON, NELLIE: *Miss Weeton: the Journal of a Governess, 1807–11*, edited by E. Hall, 1936–38, from the original manuscript, now in Wigan Central Library (Oxford University Press, 1936).

WOLLSTONECRAFT, MARY (GODWIN): *Thoughts on the Education of Daughters* (1787).

——: *A Vindication of the Rights of Woman* (1792).

WOODHAM-SMITH, CECIL: *Florence Nightingale* (Constable, 1950).

YOUNG, G. M. (ed.): *Early Victorian England* (*1830–65*) (Oxford University Press, 1934).

OFFICIAL PUBLICATIONS

Report of the Poor Law Commission, 1842.

Reports of the Health of Towns Commission, 1842 and 1845.

Second Report of Children's Employment Commission, 1843.
Report on Parliamentary Commission on Education, 1843.
Baths and Wash Houses; the History of their Rise and Progress, and a
    Description of the Lambeth Baths and Wash Houses, by G. A.
    Cape (1854).

NEWSPAPERS AND PERIODICALS
(1835-57)

Annual Register, The.
Daily News, The.
Edinburgh Review, The.
Fraser's Magazine.
Household Words.
Illustrated London News, The.
Lady's Newspaper, The.
Lancet, The.
Punch.
Saturday Review, The.
Times, The.

Belle, Assemblée, La.
Christian Lady's Magazine, The.
Eliza Cook's Journal.
Englishwoman's Domestic Magazine, The.
Female Beauty.
Juvenile, The (an illustrated penny magazine for children).
Juvenile Gleaner, The.
Juvenile Miscellany, The.
Ladies' Companion, The.
Ladies' Handbook, The.
Ladies' Monthly Museum, The.
Ladies' Pocket Magazine, The.
Ladies' Treasury, The.
Lady's Cabinet of Fashion, Music, and Romance, The.
World of Fashion, The.
Year Book of Wonders, Events, and Discoveries, The.

ANNUALS (1830-40)

Album Wreath, The.
Book of Beauty, The.
Forget-me-not, The.
Keepsake, The.

INDEX